Change Your Brain

How to Change Your Life and Break Bad Habits. Transform Your Life and Change Your Mind by Overcoming Addictions, Resolving Conflicts and Building Trust. Face Your Fears.

William Mind

Table of Contents

Introduction

Congratulations on purchasing *Change Your Brain and* thank you for doing so.

The fear of the unknown. That's one of the biggest fears we all harbor in secret, but very few would like to admit. Being in a transitional phase of life is never easy and that fear can make your brain go haywire. When your thoughts begin to feel like they're overpowering you, your sense of control begins to slip away which only causes you to feel even more frustrated and miserable at the way things are going. Embarking on a new journey with no guarantee of success is hard, and even harder to do when you don't have the right mindset to do it.

Our brain has to deal with a constant stream of negative thoughts. *What if we fail? What if we make a decision we regret for the rest of our lives? What if we make the wrong choices? What if, despite trying, we still don't succeed?* If we let it, our brains can go into overdrive, magnifying these thoughts to a point where they become almost unbearable. We're so used to being programmed to worry about what's going to happen next because of that fear of the unknown. We worry so much we forget to stop and be present because we're no longer the ones in control anymore. By the time we get to this stage, we've surrendered control to our overworked, stressed-out brain.

But what would happen if we made one small change? What if we changed our brains to stop it from focusing on the "what ifs" and the "what next?" to focus on the *"what now?"*. The minute we do that, our entire lives begin to shift. The bad habits we once carried around with us begin to fade away and make room for newer, better transformation. By simply changing our brains, we could overcome addiction, face our fears, resolve conflict, and most importantly, be present in that moment and remain in control all the way.

Every piece of advice and strategy you're about to unravel throughout the next few chapters are going to change your perspective. It's going to open your eyes to the fact that you have the power to initiate the change in your life that you want to see. You *had that power all along,* but what was holding you back from realizing that power was the negativity that was weighing down your brain. By changing your perspective, the fear of the unknown doesn't seem as powerful as it once did. You may not have the power to control everything that happens to you, but you do have the power to change your brain, change your perspective, and, ultimately, change your life.

There are plenty of books on this subject on the market, thanks again for choosing this one! Every effort was made to ensure it is full of as much useful information as possible; please enjoy!

Chapter 1: Principles to Change Your Brain and Your Life

Your brain is the organ of judgment, personality, character, and probably the characteristic that is responsible for how far we've come and all the modern-day conveniences we see around us today: *Innovation.* Innovation is a brain function. It depends on the physical health of your brain. Now, we know that our brain is involved in everything that we do. How we think, how we feel, how we act, how we make decisions, how we get along with others. When your brain *works, you work.* When your brain is troubled, you are a lot more likely to have trouble in your life too. When your brain is healthy, you're happier, healthier, wiser; you're more creative. When the brain is *not healthy,* that's when negativity becomes the dominant force in your life. So, we then ask ourselves: *Is it possible to change the brain? If so, what can we do?*

Is It Possible to Change Your Brain?

Absolutely. If science has taught us anything, it is that we're not hardwired to be a certain way for the rest of our lives, and we're not doomed by genetics. Humans are capable of some of the most incredible changes. We can literally do anything that we set our minds too, even the things that seem impossible. Our minds are our most powerful tool. It can either drive us to great heights or hold us back from ever living our dreams. Like every other muscle in the body, the mind needs to be exercised. Mental preparation is the key to boosting your motivation levels. Some of the most successful people in the world start their day every morning by mentally preparing themselves for the day ahead. They meditate, use positive affirmations, recite their goals to themselves, or even listen to motivational podcasts on their phones or tablets.

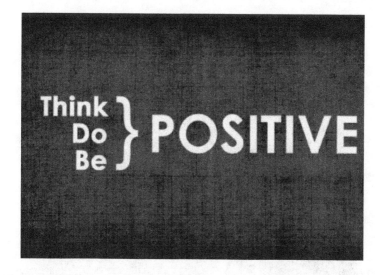

Negativity is a survival mechanism. It is the way the human mind uses it to identify what might be wrong in certain situations so we can protect ourselves from danger. For example, when we see a dangerous animal in the wild. Our brain understands that this is a negative situation where we could potentially end up getting hurt, and the survival mechanism warns us not to get involved, so we don't risk getting hurt. Negativity used as a survival mechanism is alright but allowing this mechanism to become the primary way to live is not alright. We were not meant to live in a constant state of negativity, or use it to develop connections and relationships with others. Negativity shouldn't be allowed to grow strong enough that it starts to control and take over. When you live a life where focusing on weaknesses instead of strengths becomes your default mode, you're a pessimist who will always struggle to find happiness and fulfillment in life.

Adopting new behavioral patterns and thoughts as well as recruit neutral networks that encourage new connections as well as communication pathways that can change the brain's thinking prowess over time. Repeated behavior allows the neurons of the brain to branch out and ease the information flow. When you complain repeatedly, for example, it makes it easier for the brain to keep doing the same thing next time. Repetitive complaining soon becomes habitual, and it rewires your brain, so complaining becomes even easier as you continuously indulge in this habit. In doing so, you're strengthening your brain's negative bias, making it easier to see everything that is wrong with the world around you, regardless of how many good things may be happening too.

In short, changing the brain is possible, but it needs to be *trained to think positively* if you're going to override all the negativity your brain has been accustomed to all this time.

How to Change Our Mindset and Ourselves

Your mind is your most powerful weapon of change to achieve success in everything that you do in life. If you want your life to change, to think better, do better, and achieve more, then you need to begin taking ownership of your thoughts and change the way you think. Nothing is going to change unless you make the choice to do it. To be accountable and take ownership of your mind and your thoughts. To be a problem solver instead of a downer and changing your mindset is what you need for change is going to get you there. Reframing your point of view is essentially changing your mindset. A mind over matter exercise. If you put your mind to it, you can do it.

When you change your mindset, the rest of your life will follow. You'll become an entirely new person, someone who can "step outside yourself" and observe your actions like you would if you were a third-party observer. Imagine that you were on the outside looking in, looking at the kind of person you are and the way you handle things right now. Do you like what you see? From an outsider's perspective, how would you say things could be handled better? Taking time to reflect upon yourself will bring you to a greater level of self-awareness. Only when you are able to accept and embrace what is happening and not live in denial can true change start to happen.

How do we start changing our mindsets and ourselves in the process? *By not making excuses.* Excuses do nothing for you except to distract and deter from focusing on what's important. They don't do you any good, and it is time that you dropped them. Using excuses to rationalize your decisions and reactions, to explain away behavior which you know deep down is not acceptable is not the mark of someone who is in control of their brain. Excuses will always keep you in your comfort zone and stop you from achieving success. Excuses will prevent you from ever learning how to regulate your emotions and develop empathy. Excuses, in short, are neither positive nor productive.

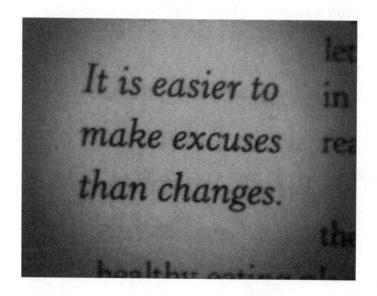

How to Illuminate Your Mind

The power of choice is something that resonates the most with our souls. The power of decision-making is one of the greatest gifts you hold. You're not the product of your genes, your family background, or your education. You are the result of your decisions. Dwight D. Eisenhower once said: *"The history of free men is never written by chance, but by choice. Their choice."* Life is about making decisions, and your success is the result of several decisions you've had to make to get to where you are.

Making decisions is not easy. Brain researcher Ernst Pöppel says that each day, we make about 20,000 decisions. Most of these decisions are done at lightning speed and unconsciously. Some decisions we adjourn to a later time (sometimes this is called procrastination). Now, your brain is a toolbox, but the problem is, most people don't really know *how to use* this toolbox. Your choices change your brain. When it comes to making decisions, whether its personal, professional or for business, the brain accesses parts of itself that we have no conscious access to. This is called the *cognitive unconscious*. This part of the brain contains the circuitry that stores data and the decisions we've made throughout our entire lives.

> "I am not a product of my circumstances. I am a product of my decisions."
> Stephen Covey

Your Choices Change Your Brain

We need to take responsibility for our brains. Some people are terrified of making decisions because they don't want to make the wrong one. However, make no mistake that *not making a decision* is *still making a decision.* When you don't make the decision, you're allowing someone else to do it for you. Today, we've got a lot of choices. You might even say we've got *too many options.* In the consumerist society, a simple trip to the grocery store could see you standing in line at the cashier with more items than you originally intended to buy. At least one or two products that weren't on your initial shopping list, to begin with. It happens to everyone, and this phenomenon is called

11

irrational buying decisions. This happens when the brain experiences a stimulus overflow and far too many options. It paralyzes the brain, and you struggle with the decision-making process.

Each time you make a decision, *why do you choose that particular decision?* That's we key question we don't always stop to ask. One study observed what happened in the human brain when people had to make decisions and compared those findings to animals who had to make similar types of decisions. One of the most fascinating takeaway from this research was how people and animals tend to make very similar choices when they find themselves in similar contexts. Moreover, the study found that the brain was the one responsible for making these decisions for them using a similar set of mechanisms. This means we can infer that the choices we make, even in a complex situation, are driven by forces that have learned long ago to solve the kinds of problems animals needed to solve like finding food, finding a mate, making friends and allies to work together with.

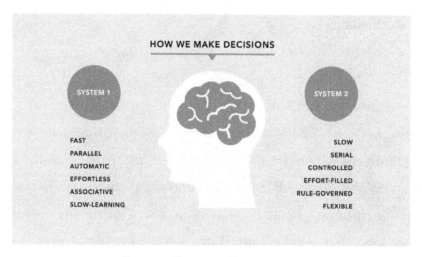

Image Source: <u>Braze.com</u>

Love, Depression, Anxiety, Fear and the Brain

For phenomena like depression, anxiety, and fear (which are three mental health conditions with close ties to each other), two key areas of the brain need to be looked at. The front part of the brain and the second part of the brain called the *limbic system,* which is where the fight or flight response resides. The front part of the brain is responsible for:

- Motivation
- Drive
- Attention
- Concentration

- Pleasure
- Mental fatigue

These functions are different from the ones affected by the limbic system. The limbic system contains an important part of the brain called the *amygdala*, which is the "threat" area of the brain. When involved, it triggers emotional responses like fear and aggression. It is responsible for controlling certain behaviors that are essential to not only humans but all mammals on this planet. We need our limbic system for self-preservation purposes, among other things like sourcing food. What's interesting about the limbic system of the human brain is that certain structures can be found in the brain structure of certain evolutionary animals too. In alligators, for example, the limbic system is there to play an important role in helping it defend its territory, eat and hunt for prey. In the human brain, the limbic system is involved in our emotional and motivational behaviors.

Emotions like depression, anxiety, and fear are complicated and could be due to several factors. Chemical imbalances in the brain, traumatic life events, genetics, or medical factors. Brain imaging studies show that depression and anxiety are connected to changes in several parts of the brain, particularly in three core areas:

- Amygdala (where emotional regulation takes place)
- Hippocampus (processes memory and regulates stress hormone)
- Thalamus (links sensory information to good and bad feelings)

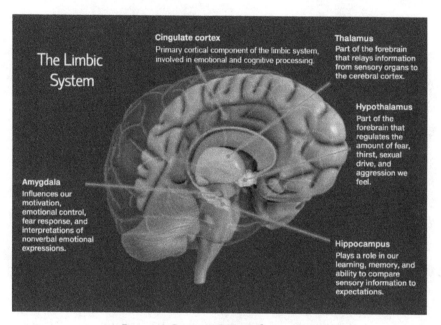

Image Source: Revelpreview

For some people, depression, anxiety, and fear are emotions they can overcome on their own. In some cases, they go back to feeling normal once the triggering event has passed. But some people struggle for years and are unable to overcome these conditions without proper treatment or medication. One major contributor to why we become consumed with our fears is because we're terrified of the "worst-case" scenario happening to us. We think about all the bad things that could possibly go wrong, and these scenarios get so built up in our heads the worry starts to grow bigger and bigger. As it does, our emotions slowly start spiraling out of control, fueling our worries even more.

As for love, well, people all over the world fall in love. They would do anything for love. They go to the ends of the earth for true love. They write poems, stories, and make movies about love and finding love. They long for love. The fight for love. They even kill in the name of love. That's how powerful this emotion is. There is no society in this world that exists without love. Love it's a primal emotion that connects us all. Whether its platonic, romantic, or familial, love is not always perfect. When love it's great, it's wonderful. But, as we all know, love is not always a happy emotion. So, what happens to the brain when we experience love? Why, despite being sometimes a painful emotion, do we still long for it so badly?

Love is something we feel in our hearts, but science shows that love actually begins in the brain. When we experience love, our brain is hijacked by a concoction of hormones, including serotonin, dopamine, and vasopressin, that induce a sense of euphoria. Dopamine, the hormone that makes you feel good, is also responsible for storing long-term memory. But when love goes wrong, it can trigger anxiety and depression for the broken heart. Falling in love and investing all your emotions in another person can be a scary prospect for anyone. But for someone who is *already dealing* with anxiety, it can be downright frightening. No matter how old we may be or at what stage of life we are at, giving your heart to someone is a frightening prospect because you are opening yourself to the possibility of being hurt. For someone who is living with anxiety, that fear is magnified tenfold.

There's a lot of things that could impact our perception of love. If that perception is negative, it's likely as a result of failed relationships you experienced before, maybe something traumatic happened while you were in a relationship. Even seeing your loved ones and friends go through a negative love experience can cause your perception to sway toward the negative. When you're dealing with anxiety, that fear of having the relationship fail can haunt your every waking moment. It isn't easy living a life in which you are constantly worried and afraid that something bad is going to happen. When it involves someone that you care about, it can be almost unbearable because the very thought of losing the one that you love is too painful to bear. Sometimes, after the breakdown of a relationship, anxiety can make it difficult for you to move on and deal with it. This only further emphasizes the need to change your brain, change your mindset, and develop a positive outlook.

You Cannot Change What You Do Not Measure

Before you undertake the journey to change your brain and change your mindset and your life, there's something else you need to do, too: *Be accountable.* You'll hear this term thrown around a lot in the workplace a lot, yet very few people understand what it truly means. Accountability is often associated with our professional life, but it needs to spill over into your personal life now too, especially when you're trying to initiate a change for the better. Why? Because *you cannot change what you do not measure.* If there's no measurement or some type of gauge as to how well you're doing and what kind of progress you've made, how will you know what needs to be changed? Or what areas need to be improved on?

If you think about it, all of us change all the time. It's not just people that change too. Everything in the world goes through change. It is the very nature of existence. Some people undergo more positive change than others because they are accountable. An example of what happens when you're not accountable for your life and your actions is when you notice that your life is changing for the worst. It's filled with more negativity, unhappiness, despair, depression, anxiety, more bad episodes than you'd like to go through, relationships that get lost along the way. When it feels like your life has spiraled out of control, that's because you're not accountable for what's going on. When you're not accountable, you're not in control. If you don't start doing something to change your life, what is going to become of it?

Being accountable and taking responsibility for the changes that happen in your life is one of the first few steps needed to push for the positive change you need to so. It's not difficult to begin either. When you start your day, start by picking one virtue that you want to work on for the day and go with that. For example, today, you're going to work on forgiveness. Or you could choose to work on happiness, mindfulness, patience, gratitude; the list goes on. You would then go about your day as you ordinarily would, and at the end of the day and reflect on how your day went. Hold yourself accountable for the actions that happened. Did your intention to work on forgiveness go as well as you hoped? If not, why not? What can you do tomorrow that would make it better? What can you do to improve? If it helps, enlist the help of someone you trust to hold you accountable for your actions of the day. Tell them in the morning what virtue you intend to focus on, and have them check in with you to see how well you're doing. Let's say a colleague annoyed you at work today and you're still mad at him for it. Your friend, partner, or family member could then point out, *"But you said you were going to practice forgiveness today? Why aren't you forgiving your colleague?"*. They'll be there to remind of the moments when you need to be accountable but you're not doing it.

The thing about change is, you don't *see it happening*. When you start exercising for the first time, it doesn't seem like you're getting fitter or stronger from one day to the next. When you're saving money and set a target amount you would like to see in your bank account, you don't see that happening in a week, a month, or a year. That's one of the reasons why change is so hard. We don't see it happening, so it doesn't *feel* like anything is changing. That's even more reason why you need to be accountable. It's about being responsible for your choices and your decisions instead of letting your brain and your emotions decide for you. If you measure every single thing you do each day to change toward your goal, and when you look back on that progress 3 months from now or 6 months from now, that's when you see how far you've come. So, start by picking one habit each time that you want to work on overcoming. One habit that you want to change for the better. Or you could pick one good habit that you want to start. Go with one first and let your brain focus on just one thing at a time to minimize distraction.

How Positive Thinking *Will* Change Your Life

What do you think the happiest and most successful people think about all day long? The answer is simple: *Most of the time, healthy and happy people think about what they want and what they can do to get it.* They don't think about this *all* the time because there are other responsibilities to attend to, but most of the time, these are the dominant thoughts that will occupy their mind. What they want. How to get it. They do this because they understand the power of positive thinking and how important it is to develop that positive mindset.

Your positive attitude and thinking are the two most important qualities you can have if you want to change your life. When you keep thinking and talking about all the things you want and how to get it, you feel like you're in control of your life. Subsequently, you feel happier because your brain is releasing endorphins each time you think about the things you want. The word "thinking" can mean an extensive number of things. The way that we think shapes the world around us. A person who thinks positively tends to attract opportunities and success because of their optimistic outlook and ability to see the silver lining where others would be tempted to give up. A person who thinks negatively tends to experience a higher degree of failure. The way we think influences our outlook on life and to bring about great change for the better requires a shift in the way that we think from this point onwards.

When something happens bad or unexpected happens to you, there are two ways you can handle the situation. You can choose to put a positive spin on what might be a very difficult situation, or you could be defeated by it, complain, and end up making yourself and everyone else around you miserable in the process. Choosing positivity is not something you do as a one-off. It is something that you need to practice every single day. There's a quote by Wayne Dyer, who says: *"If you change the way you look at things, the things you look at will change."*

Here's an example of a scenario. Think about a time when the water went off in your house. You had no water to boil, take a shower with, wash your clothes or do any of the stuff you normally would. You know the water is going to come back on at some point, and there will be plenty of it. But for those couple of hours, you're inconvenienced. Some people might look at this negatively and complain about how difficult it is and how their routine has been disrupted. They could be so bothered by it that it spoils their mood for an entire day. Then there are others, who might think that's okay, it's a minor setback and the water is going to come back on later. Now, we're so used to having running water in our homes every day that we don't stop to realize how fortunate we are. There are so many in less fortunate countries who have to survive on less. In Africa, some people have to survive on less than 5 liters of water per day for everything, and that includes drinking, cooking, cleaning, washing their clothes, taking a bath. What most of us use in one shower session is what others rely on for an entire day to survive. If you think about it from that perspective, we are incredibly fortunate, so a couple of hours without water is nothing to complain about when we know there are people out there who don't even know where their next source of fresh water supply is coming from. That's what a change in perspective can do. Your thinking sets the stage for your life. When you change your outlook, you change your entire life. That's how powerful a tool the mind can be. When your mind focuses on nothing but misery and the problems that you're plagued with, your life and outlook are going to mirror that train of thought. If you were to focus on the positives, however, and focus on the solutions instead of the problem, you become the type of person who can still smile in the face of adversity.

perspective...

How Can I Train My Brain to Be Positive?

When you change your perception from positive to negative, you don't just change yourself. You could possibly change the people around you too. Becoming more resilient against negativity is like a snowball effect because once you are more resilient, you find that you feel less tense, your blood pressure is lowered because your levels of stress have decreased, your body feels a lot more relaxed and aches less, and you don't fall ill as often anymore because you feel good about yourself. That's the power of positivity already at work

- **Saying Thank You:** Make saying *"Thank you"* the first activity of the day as soon as you open your eyes in the morning. You're alive, and you've got a whole day ahead of you to make something good out of it. Being alive is a blessing that we take for granted the most and the simple act of saying thank you each morning will train your brain to appreciate your life that much more. The act of saying thank you gives value to your life and it changes your perception.

- **Using Humor:** One component that makes positivity easier if you learn to use humor. Learn to laugh at yourself and laugh with others. Even the most miserable situations can be helped with a little humor. It is the medicine that keeps despair at bay. You're not denying the misery you feel, but simply cultivating a different relationship with it. Instead of letting that unhappy moment define you, you're making the choice to put a positive spin on it and use that humor to develop inner strength. Laughter, real genuine laughter, is one of the best remedies you could feed your body because laughter releases dopamine, a chemical that invokes feelings of pleasure and happiness in our bodies. When you are laughing, it is impossible to feel any kind of stress or tension during the process, and it is impossible to feel negative when you're having a good, honest laugh.

- **Keeping a Gratitude Journal** - Writing down a list of all that you're grateful for can be a helpful exercise in training your brain to be more positive. Practicing gratitude is easy and something that you can do every single day. A good way to start is by keeping a gratitude journal, and you can start with something simple by writing down every day one or more things that happened to you today that you are very grateful for. With so much happening around you each day, it's easy to overlook the good things you encountered during the day. Aim to write down one thing you're grateful for at the very least, and five if you can manage it. Writing it down helps you to actively remember that you do have reasons to be grateful for, and each time you feel negativity threatening to take over, open your journal and read the list of all the things you have to be grateful for.

- **Smile:** Another facet of positivity is to smile. Get up in the morning and smile at yourself in the mirror. Smile as you head out the door and off to work. Smile at the people you meet along the way. Smile because it's a powerful thing. Mother Theresa once said: *"Peace begins with a smile."* She also said: *"We shall never know all the good a simple smile can do."*

26

- **Positive Affirmations:** Positive affirmations were underestimated for a long time, that is until research suggested that they are powerful tools that could significantly decrease stress and enhance problem-solving abilities. It's easier to do this when we learn to pay attention and be grateful for the small things. We're all guilty of only focusing on big acts of gratitude and forget about the little things we have to be thankful for. For example, getting a cup of coffee at work when you're on your break or when you have your lunch at the local cafe. You see this as part of your daily routine, but think about how many people around the world are either starving or not as fortunate as you are to enjoy a nice, warm cup of coffee and a warm meal to fill their bellies.

- **Embrace Diversity:** No matter who they are or where they come from, everyone is important. Regardless of the country of origin, race, religion, age, sexual preference, gender, everyone matters. Defining people by what they are rather than who they are is how you form judgments and negative biases toward each other. Instead, if we took the time to know people that are different from our usual experiences and respect them for their unique individuality, that cultivates an open mind and, with it, a more positive attitude. At the end of the day, we all want the same things. We want love, happiness, safety, security, being with family, raising children well. As humans, we agree on these same basic principles. It's okay that we all have different opinions. What is *not* okay is when we insist that others should go along with what we think is best. We need to be open to the opinions of others, to see what it is that makes them passionate or excited. You may not agree or prefer their opinions, but you learn to appreciate the fact that they do. In doing so, we can learn a lot from people who are so different from us and it is these experiences that all come together to help shape a positive perception of the world.

It's not always possible to be positive because life is not perfect. There will be moments in your life that are downright negative. In your darkest days, it might require a lot more work to find your way back to the positive place again. You'll need to be willing to do what it takes to get back to that. This world is an amazing place, and if you're reading this, you've got a lot in your life to be grateful for. You simply need to find your way back to that happy place, and that's what you'll learn to do throughout the course of the next few chapters.

Chapter 2: Improving the Brain

Changing your mindset is entirely up to you. It is not only possible, but it's also *necessary* to revolutionize your life and witness visible change happening at last. Your progress begins now. Not tomorrow, not next week, not next month, not a year from now. But right *now*.

Right now, it's probably hard to imagine any kind of positive change happening in your life if you've been struggling with negativity for a while. It's going to take a lot of inner strength to pick yourself up and try to put your life back together. Change never comes easy, and trying to change something as strong and powerful as a brain that has been trapped in old habits is even harder. But that's *exactly why* you should do it. Learning to change your brain is going to one of the best decisions you decide to make today. By learning to conquer your mind, you can change your life because that goal that you've given yourself is the laser-sharp focus that you need. Having that goal to focus on puts things in perspective and eliminates distractions once you realize that they serve no purpose.

Can the Brain Rewire Itself?

How Do We Improve Our Brains?

Neuroplasticity is an idea that is widely accepted today, and scientists have proven many times over that our brains are dynamic and adaptable. The human brain is so powerful that can alter its structure, even in those who experienced severe neurological afflictions. It is absolutely incredible to think that those who were dealing with recovery from mental illness, stroke, and cerebral palsy could train other areas of their brain through consistent and repetitive physical and mental activities.

Norman Doidge M.D., author of _The Brain That Changes Itself: Stories of Personal Triumph from the Frontiers of Brain Science_, adamantly stated that the brain is more than capable of rewiring itself and forming new neural pathways of needed. However, you need to be the one that initiates this change. It requires repetition and consistent effort over a prolonged period to reinforce this. By repeatedly engaging in positive activities and thinking positive thoughts, you can rewire the way your brain thinks and start strengthening the areas of the brain that stimulate positive emotions. Think of it the way you would with exercise. To see any kind of physical change in your body, you need to keep going at it for a sustained period. Change doesn't happen overnight. Your brain is a muscle that you're not about to exercise and if you keep going, it is only going to get stronger with time.

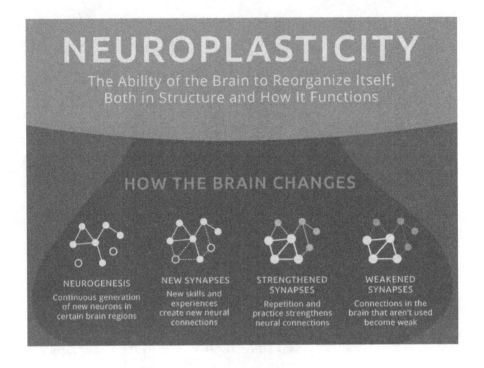

Image Source: <u>Neurogym</u>

Learning Changes the Brain

Every time you engage in a new behavior or activity, your brain generates new neural pathways and form new connections with other neurons. Imagine your brain is like a highway, and the neurons are the many alternative routes you can take to arrive at your destination. This means that if one neural pathway is blocked, it's not the end of the road. There's always another avenue. Your brain takes in all the positive new experiences it encounters, and as you work on strengthening the neural pathways, the synapses start to grow close together. Whenever a new electrical signal activates the synapses, it bridges the gap between them, and they grow even closer together. The closer your synapses are, the faster the information transmits. Therefore, as the brain's positive thought synapses start to grow closer, positive thoughts begin to win in the face against negative thoughts because they travel much faster. So yes, it is absolutely possible to rewire the brain and improve it the way we want, *but it requires action on our part* to get it done. Change is not going to happen by itself unless we do something about it.

6 Ways to Shift Your Mindset and Embrace Change

The working relationship you have between you and your mind is the most important relationship you could have. When you collaborate and work together with your mind instead of against it, when you tell it what you want, you *get the results you want*. If you can make this relationship work, there's no limit to the things you can achieve. If you change your brain is this simple way by shifting your mindset, you can easily achieve success at every level across the board. No question about it.

To shift your mindset, you need to first understand four important things about the way the mind works:

- **1:** Your mind does *exactly* what it *thinks you want it to do*. The mind is programmed to help you survive and therefore, it is always acting in what it *thinks* is your best interest.

- **2:** The way you feel every day comes down to two things. One, the words that you say to yourself. Two, the scenarios you visualize in your head. If the words you use are negative and the scenarios you envision are negative, then you're always going to be feeling miserable until you do something to turn that around.

- **3:** Your mind is hardwired for pleasure. It is designed to move toward the greatest source of pleasure and simultaneously move away from pain.

- **4:** The mind loves familiarity and routine. It is programmed to repeatedly go back to the same behavior and the same habits it has grown comfortable with.

Your mind is constantly listening to the language you tell it. If you say, *"I'm so stressed and this workload is more than I can manage, I can't handle all this pressure"* you are telling your mind you *don't want to do this.* As soon as your mind thinks you don't want to do something, it's going to encourage you to procrastinate, to find excuses, to slack off, and perhaps even refuse to do the task at all. Your mind is so tuned in to the words you use that even the slightest hint of negativity immediately puts it on the path to doing everything it can to avoid difficulty. It's not just our thoughts we need to be aware of, but the words that we say too. The words and the language that you use to describe yourself, your life, and the people around you shape the reality that you live in. The words you speak hold immense power in them. With a few simple words, you can either lift yourself up or bring yourself crashing down, defeated and demotivated. A few spoken words are all it takes to either give someone hope or destroy their self- esteem. If you believe that you are surrounded by loving, supportive people, that life is good and full of possibilities and you vocalize that, you're cultivating such an environment for yourself using the power of your words.

Take a good look at where your life is right now. The habits and the behaviors you engage in. If you're not getting the results you want, then it's clear you're not working together with your mind, and that needs to change. You're not communicating or training your mind in the direction you want it to go. You need to start talking to your mind in a positive way, even if you don't believe what you're saying at first. Imagine you're running five miles and by the second mile, you're already tired and you feel like stopping. If you're telling yourself, *"This is boring. I want to stop. I hate running why am I doing this"*, you're not going to finish that run. But if you tell yourself, *"This is good. I love running. I can feel myself getting stronger. Two miles down, only three more to go this is easy I've got this,"* you're collaborating with your mind, telling it what you want it to do and it's going to carry you all the way to the end of your run.

Remember, your mind is hardwired to stay away from pain, and it will do anything to avoid anything it perceives as difficult. To shift your mindset and embrace change, you need to be very specific about the words you say and the things you do. To become the better version of yourself and tap into all that potential buried underneath a mindset that has been holding you back for far too long. You've yearned for too long to be like those successful individuals you look up to, and this is where you take your very first step in that direction.

The mindset you choose to adopt is entirely up to you, but it is extremely important that you choose the right mindset to chart the course for the rest of your life. There's no shortage of research and evidence that clearly shows how the mindset you choose to adopt can radically alter the way you learn, how resilient you are, how you handle stress, and the way you create the success you achieve in your life. To shift your mindset, there are six specific steps that need to be carried out, all six of which are designed to open your mind and train to embrace the necessary change needed, no matter how difficult that change may be.

Step 1: Learning to Meditate

Now that we know the mind determines the experiences in life, what can we do about it? Often, we're just focused on taking care of the physical part of ourselves that we neglect to remember our minds need just as much attention and care because we don't realize the extent of what being weighed down by stress, worry, and anxiety can do to us. These negative emotions are so powerful that in extreme cases, they can even manifest themselves physically. The art of meditation has a long history to it. The act of sustaining that prolonged period of inward focus where it's just you and your mind can be an incredible experience. However, a calm mind does not necessarily mean that your brain is on a break. Surprisingly enough, the act of meditation has a measurable effect on our brain's activity.

Consistent meditation disables the distractions we face by filtering it before it starts to bottleneck. Think of it as a river dam that ensures the right amount of water gets flowed down to households, industries, and agriculture. Meditation, in the same way, filters the less important data that we are exposed to and sends only the necessary and important info into our brain. In other words, it helps us determine what information should we focus on and what we do not need to focus on that may cause chronic anxiety. Researches from Rutgers University and the University of California also conducted research relating to mindfulness meditation and the effects on cortisol. The study shows that consistent meditation reduced cortisol dramatically, with some results showing at least a 50% drop. Daily meditation for even 3 minutes is effective for the brain. Meditation is like the firefighters you call to extinguish this hormone that brings in so many diseases that can protect your health and happiness.

Sometime in the 1970s, Harvard physician Herbert Benson looked at the behaviors of the patients visiting him due to stress-related disorders such as anxiety. His observation led him to look at ways that he could counteract this association, simultaneously revolutionizing the mental care industry and helping people. Dr. Benson's discovery was the connection between the mind and body through meditation. It slowed metabolism, reduced the heart rate, resulted in measured breathing and quieter brainwave activity. All of this combined brought out the right foundations for healing. Another study conducted by Dr. Sara Lazar in 2005 was a landmark study that showed the brains of those who meditated were much thicker and had more folds and surface area in their prefrontal cortexes. This study is used now by various neuroscientific and psychological researches as the go-to foundational study for other mental health issues such as depression. Those who meditate, even for 10 to 15 minutes a day, are usually anxiety-free, happy, and healthy.

Our thoughts come and go, and through meditation, we can at least focus on the various emotions with a more structured mind without needing to chase the rabbit down its never-ending hole. Through meditation, we can build our mental muscles and allow us to understand the deepest levels of our mind and connect to our thoughts, emotions, and mind. If you are new to meditation, you might begin by clearing your mind and focusing your attention on your breathing. As you do this, your brain's natural rhythm, which is called *brain waves,* begin to shift. *Beta Waves,* which is the choppy rhythm that is triggered when there's active thought happening, steps aside and makes way for slower *Alpha Waves*. These *Alpha Waves* are more prevalent during the moments when you feel most relaxed. When relaxed, the brain then begins to produce stronger waves known as *Gamma Waves*. These waves are associated with deep concentration.

When scientists compared the brains of Buddhist monks with new meditators, they discovered that the region of the brain associated with empathy was a lot more pronounced in the monks who had been regularly meditating for years. The higher Alpha waves in the minds of these meditators reduced the number of negative emotions experienced. Studies conducted have discovered that after 8-weeks of meditation, gray matter in the brain was denser in areas associated with learning, emotional regulation, and memory processing. The amygdala, however, which deals with blood pressure and stress, experienced a decrease in brain matter.

Meditation is probably the single most important skill you can learn in a world today where stressful stimuli come at you from all angles. Human beings are the species with the most highly developed brain on the planet, and because of that, we're given the gift of being able to create things. We create technology. We create inventions that make our lives a little bit easier. We've helped to shape the planet into what it is today. Our brain has so much power; we can even *reshape our reality* by simply learning how to quiet the mind and change our brains. When you no longer overthink things or you do not have to worry or have the feeling of constant fear, or when you stop worrying endlessly about what the future holds, you get to experience a silence that is intoxicating. Meditation allows your mind to explore this side of your natural state, the stillness that is true and pure.

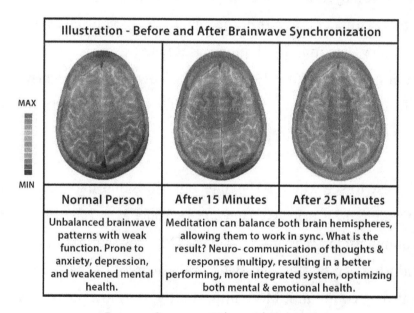

Illustration - Before and After Brainwave Synchronization		
Normal Person	After 15 Minutes	After 25 Minutes
Unbalanced brainwave patterns with weak function. Prone to anxiety, depression, and weakened mental health.	Meditation can balance both brain hemispheres, allowing them to work in sync. What is the result? Neuro- communication of thoughts & responses multipy, resulting in a better performing, more integrated system, optimizing both mental & emotional health.	

Image Source: Hingori Sutras

Step 2: Make Personal Development a Priority for Yourself

Life is always changing, and if you don't change along with it, you're going to find yourself stuck in one place while everyone else around you seems to be moving forwards and upwards. Personal development is the way we upgrade ourselves. It is the way we learn, the way we develop new skills, the way we learn to understand how our minds work. In short, personal development ensures that you're not left behind while life passes you by, taking the opportunities you missed out on along with it. Think of it as a training technique for your brain, where each new personal development is a new way of teaching your brain how to perform better. All the new skills you learn will help you get from Point A to Point B in a lot less time so you can then *make the most out of your time.*

It's easy to see who are the ones out there that make personal development a priority. They are the ones who have achieved monumental success in their lives. The ones that we look up to and aspire to be, the ones who are successes in the industries that they command. More importantly, they are the ones who did not let any obstacle stand in their way and hold them back. This is the one thing that sets them apart, and it was having the right mindset. That's all it took for them to stand out.

Now, personal development can only be achieved if self-awareness exists. Before you can even begin comprehending and relating to your internal self and external environment, you must first understand yourself. Self-awareness is the ability to clearly see all the different aspects that contribute to the personality that you have. It means paying attention to the way that your body responds to certain triggers, how it feels and reacts when it experiences certain emotions, and generally how you respond to the stimuli of your surroundings. Being someone who's self-aware means you're less likely to be caught off guard or unprepared when something doesn't go your way. Developing an acute level of self-awareness is how you stop yourself from repeating the mistakes of the past, and how you prevent yourself from reacting inappropriately when you feel overwhelmed or under pressure.

Personal development is also about what you choose to fill your mind with. Just because you left school a long time ago, it does not mean your education has come to an end. The number one problem that many people struggle with when it comes to shifting their mindset is that they think they are done with education. As a result, they no longer try as hard to learn, not realizing that learning is a lifelong process that never stops. Therefore, we continue having a lot of problems. We have problems with relationships, our finances, our career, our social skills, we have trouble with forgiveness. We have problems because we *don't make personal development a priority*.

There's a lot of different areas of personal development that you could look into. Love, people, time, money, education, friendships, career, the list goes on. But the most important areas of personal development you could focus on *yourself first*. To focus on creating the best version of yourself and working on the areas of your life which may not be so great just yet and figuring out what you can do to make it better. Focus on growing as a person, expanding your reach and capabilities, pushing past the boundaries that once made you uncomfortable to see just how far you can go. Your personal development is an *investment*. A quote by Jim Rohn tells us that we need to work on ourselves *harder* than we work at our jobs, and that quote holds the absolute truth. By working on yourself, you're giving yourself the tools and skills you need to make you a more capable and valuable individual. This is the kind of mindset that takes you from where you are to where you want to be.

Step 3: Retraining Your Brain by Noticing 3 Positive Changes Per Day

Whether this change turns out positive or otherwise, comes down to the way you handle yourself, your emotions, and the way that you relate to others in a high-pressured or challenging situation. Our brain is a gift. If we don't cherish our brains and take care of it the way it deserves, it won't be long before we start to break down emotionally and mentally. You won't feel it at first or realize that it is happening until it's too late to do anything about it. Your mind is the vehicle that you are going to journey through life with, and you must take care of it both on the inside and out for better health physically, emotionally, and of course, mentally.

We possess a natural ability to be aware, yet it is one of the most overlooked tools we have readily available to help us cope with the everyday stressors we encounter with our daily routine. To begin training the brain to recognize positivity, we need to tap into our senses, thoughts, and current emotions, training our minds to pay attention to our surroundings. Can you name three positive things that happened to you today? That's all you need to start with. If you can name more than three, that's wonderful! Name as many as you'd like. As you go about your day, use awareness and mindfulness to notice everything that's happening around you. The minute something good happens, tell your brain, *"Oh, look! That's something positive that happened!"* and keep doing this repeatedly until you've trained your brain to easily recognize the signs of positivity.

This daily habit won't just rewire your brain and train it to focus on the good rather than it bad, but it also creates a sense of gratitude and peace. It's impossible not to feel happy when you see something good happening. Remember how the brain likes pleasure over pain? This is how you train it to actively seek out positive experiences.

Step 4: Focusing on Your Short, Medium and Long-Term Vision

Your vision is the better life that you see for yourself. The life that you want to help create. For example, you could say, *"I envision a life where I am the one in control of my mind and my brain."* A vision is about the "big picture." That's what separates it from a goal, which is more tangible, measurable, and quantifiable. Goals are the steps that help you accomplish your *vision*. We all have different dreams, different visions of what our golden years would look like. But for this mindset shift to work, you need to focus on the vision that works for *you*.

"Your vision will only start to become clearer when you start looking into your own heart." Those wise words were spoken

by Carl Jung. When you look into your heart, what kind of life do you see for yourself? What would it be like to live a life where you're the one in charge of your destiny, not your thoughts? You need to make a list of what your short, medium and long-term vision are for this journey you're about to begin and to stay focused on your vision; you need to make *visualization* a regular habit. Visualization is a mental exercise, which means you are going to start working at it before you can begin grasping the benefits of this method.

The act of visualization is more than just being able to paint a pretty picture in your mind that brings a smile to your face. It's about connecting your present self now to the person in that not too distant future, which will then lead you to start thinking about how and what you can do to make that vision come true. By knowing what you want in the future, you can start thinking about the action steps which need to be taken right now to get you one step closer. The more details you can put into this visualized image, the better you'll be able to think about how you're going to make it happen.

Even better, if you really want to hone in on your vision and stay as focused as possible, consider creating a vision board of your dream life and put it somewhere in your home where you could look at it every day. A vision board serves as a reminder that this is what you're working towards. On this board could be a collection of everything that motivates and inspires you to keep going, and you'll know you have created the perfect vision board when you feel moved to take some action each time that you look at it.

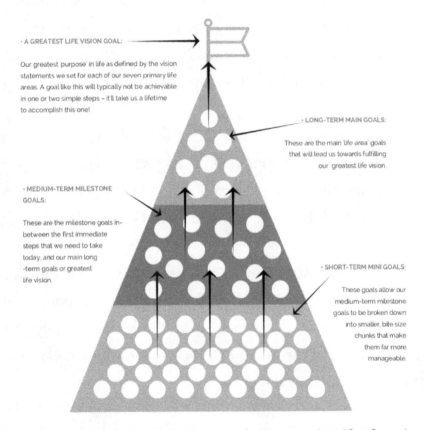

- A GREATEST LIFE VISION GOAL:

Our greatest 'purpose' in life as defined by the vision statements we set for each of our seven primary life areas. A goal like this will typically not be achievable in one or two simple steps – it'll take us a lifetime to accomplish this one!

- LONG-TERM MAIN GOALS:

These are the main 'life area' goals that will lead us towards fulfilling our greatest life vision.

- MEDIUM-TERM MILESTONE GOALS:

These are the milestone goals in-between the first immediate steps that we need to take today, and our main long-term goals or greatest life vision.

- SHORT-TERM MINI GOALS:

These goals allow our medium-term milestone goals to be broken down into smaller, bite size chunks that make them far more manageable.

Image Source: from Kain Ramsay's "Dynamic Life Planning Workbook"

Step 5: Do the Dirty Work Yourself

If you want something done right, you've got to do it yourself, but if you don't know how to do it. The next smartest thing to do is to work with someone who does. The new mindset you need to adopt now is this: *No matter what you want to accomplish in life, if you want to succeed, you need to get comfortable with being uncomfortable.* In other words, you're going to have to learn to be okay doing things you don't want to do. Bringing about positive changes in life is going to be hard work. You might have to do things your brain does not necessarily like (since it favors ease). Anything that is worth having in life will require that you do things you don't want to do. That sounds hard right from the start, but the thing is, it *doesn't have to be.*

You don't need to take your thoughts seriously. You don't need to pay attention or engage with every thought that pops into your head, especially if the negative ones. You don't need to perceive every thought you have as the truth. You are *not your thoughts.* Treat your mind like a suggestion box, and you get to choose which thoughts are going to benefit you most while discarding the rest. When your mind tries to suggest a negative thought, simply thank it for the suggestion, and then move on. When most people reject discomfort, what they are actually rejecting is their *perception* of discomfort. Since your beliefs determine your response, what you choose to believe is within your control. Your brain is no doubt going to try and talk you out of doing any hard work because it does not want to venture out of its comfort zone. But anytime you feel discomfort, it means you're doing something *right*. When you feel discomfort, it's a signal that you should *keep going* because you're training your brain to get stronger with every challenge you force it to overcome.

Overcoming your brain is something you're going to have to work hard on, and you're going to have to do the "dirty work" on your own. No one else can do it for you.

Step 6: Listen to Trusted Outside Perspectives

Not all problems can be solved alone. Sometimes, you need to know when to ask for help or when to seek the counsel of others. It's important to learn how to talk about your struggles because you can't avoid problems and issues forever. There is no "wishing it would go away" or sweeping it under the rug and pretending like it doesn't exist. The more you ignore your problems, the harder they will be to fix. The more you try to run away from your troubles, the harder it will be for your brain to try and shift its mindset. Having someone you trust to talk about your feelings with can feel good. Open the door to all those feelings you've been holding inside and let it burst forth.

Talking about it out loud is a way of channeling the stress externally, so the tension is not built-up inside you. It is difficult to change a mind that is too consumed and focused on nothing else but stress, so that problem needs to be fixed first before you work on anything else.

Talking things out and learning to trust the perspectives of others can be a helpful exercise in reducing the stressful thoughts you have since talking things over helps you see things in a different light. Sometimes the person you're talking too could put things into perspective and give you the clarity you need to find a workable solution to your problem. There's nothing that reminds you of how much you have to be grateful for quite like connecting with the people you love. The people who love you in return. The ones who make you feel safe, secure, and understood. Connecting with your loved ones is a natural stress reliever for both the mind and body. They may not be able to fix your stress entirely, but being in their company, talking about something else other than your worries, maybe even laughing and having a good time, can wash away all the unpleasant thoughts you were struggling to shake.

When things start to feel too much, seek comfort in connecting with loved ones. Find someone you can trust and talk to them about how you feel. Sometimes it helps to just get it off your chest. Learning to trust others, their advice, judgment, and perspective have the additional benefit of encouraging the use of positive speech. Which is especially beneficial in a romantic relationship. Learning to talk about the difficult things can be much easier if both you adopt the approach to only use positive language during the conversation. Being mindful of how damaging and powerful the wrong choice of words can be, let's think carefully before you speak instead of just blurting out the first thing that comes to mind. Phrases like *"I hear what you're saying and I value what you have to say"* or *"I know this is difficult to talk about, but I'm here to support you let's work through this together"* are examples of some great positive language that can be used to help control the conversation and steer it in the right direction. It minimizes the chances of things escalating and getting out of hand. You're also less likely to experience those moments when you wish you could take back what you said.

Chapter 3: 10 *Other* Things You Can Do to Change Your Brain

What would life be like if you could overcome your anxieties? Your fears? Your depression? Pretty incredible, most likely. The human brain is an extraordinary thing. What would your life be like if you were the one in control of your brain again, instead of the other way around? You've probably tried several times before this to overcome your brain but had very little success. That's because, like most people, you probably focused on *addressing the problem* rather than tackle the underlying issue that causes the problem in the first place. In this case, it is our thoughts and our perceptions that are creating trouble.

We think we've discovered all there is to know about it, yet scientists continue to learn new and fascinating facts about the way our mind works.

1: Believe You Can Change Your Brain

It's time to start believing in the power of your thoughts. Your thoughts can be a powerful driver, one that – *if harnessed correctly* – will drive you all the way to your goals and the life that you want. The power of believing in yourself can give you the determination and the ability to do things you would never have thought you could before. Believing that your brain can change will bring you so much desire to succeed that you become willing to do whatever it takes to make it happen. More importantly, you will no longer feel tempted to give in to that desire to quit because you're now fueled by positive thoughts and energy which feeds into your soul. By *believing* you have the power to change your mind because you're stronger than you give yourself credit for, it turns out you *can indeed change your brain.*

Carol Dweck talks about the incredible power of believing in yourself by highlighting how children who were taught that they didn't know how to pass a test or solve a problem *yet* were the ones who were more willing to learn. By simply using the words "not yet," the children display greater levels of confidence and showed a willingness to persist. In short, the words *yet* and *not yet* changed the perception and the mindsets of the students. Each time you push beyond your comfort zone and show a willingness to try something new, you're forming stronger new connections in the brain. As you repeatedly engage in this kind of behavior, those connections only grow stronger with time, thus changing the structure of the brain. All through the incredible power of self-belief.

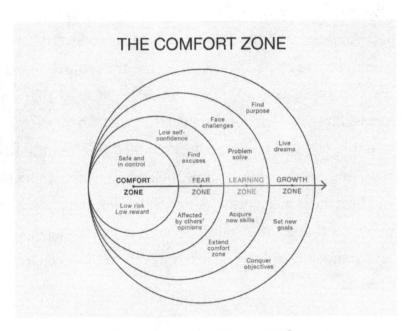

Image Source: I Love Ugly

2: Regular Exercise

We all know that exercise makes us feel better. But if you asked us why most people would be stumped for an accurate answer. We assume it's because we're burning off stress or boosting endorphins. But the real reason we feel so good when we exercise is *that exercising* makes the brain function at its best.

In today's technology-driven plasma screen the world, it's easy to forget that we were born to move. Nowadays, we spend most of our time sitting behind the desk or lying on the couch, and we have basically removed a lot of movement from our lives. This has become a norm in the past century, but we must remember that we didn't evolve for this type of sedentary lifestyle, we evolved as hunter-gatherers.

Exercise has always been associated with losing weight more so than anything else, but that only touches the tip of the iceberg. There's so much to be gained from physical activity, yet most of the incredible benefits are overlooked because most of us are only focused on one thing: *Weight loss.* That is it. But dig deeper, and you'll realize exercise is one of the few activities that have an immediate, positive benefit for the brain. This includes an immediate improvement in your focus and your mood. What happens to your brain when you exercise can protect it from different mental health conditions like depression, dementia, or Alzheimer's disease. That is how powerful physical activity can be. By simply moving your body, that one act has immediate, long-lasting and protective benefits for your brain which last for the rest of your life. That's incredible. But *why is exercise the most transformative thing that we can do for our brains?*

By now, we've established that the brain is both a powerful and the most complex structure known to mankind. In a book called _Spark_ by Jordan Ratey published in 2008, he proved that exercises and more effects on your brain than any other parts of your body. Exercise tends to be a secret recipe to boost your motivation, focus, and memory. Almost as though it were a magic pill that instantly boosts your brain capabilities. The human brain is not a fixed organ that cannot be changed. Quite the contrary, it is a highly adaptable organ that changed exactly like any other muscle on your body. When you lift weights, for example, you strengthen your arms, and the more you use it, the stronger and more flexible your arms muscles become.

Our brain is the most important organ in your body. Everything we do, think, and feel is governed by how our brain cells or neurons are connected to each other. They connect to each other through _neurotransmitters,_ specifically the following three:

- **Dopamine** - This neurotransmitter that's responsible for your motivation, and it keeps your brain looking for rewards, so you stay motivated. If you ever been hit by a burst of inspiration to do anything, it's because of the dopamine in your brain. On the other hand, when you feel a lack of desire to do _anything,_ your dopamine levels are running low. Research reveals that exercise has proven highly effective as a natural booster for your dopamine levels.

- **Serotonin** - Think of this neurotransmitter as your brain's policeman. It influences your mood, anger, and aggressiveness, and helps to keep your brain activity under control. In other words, if you feel anxious and depressed or stressed out, that's probably because your serotonin level is low. Exercise, as research shows, is a natural way of boosting the levels of serotonin in your brain without having to rely on any drugs to do it.

- **Norepinephrine** - This neurotransmitter is responsible for your attention and focus. When you struggle to do either, it's like your norepinephrine levels are low.

If your first response is *"I'm so busy where do I find the time to exercise?"*, you'll be happy to learn that there is a way to maximize your exercise benefits in the least amount of time possible. High-intensity aerobic exercise is the best way to go. This involves running jump rope, anything to get your heart rate up all the way up to 80% of its maximum rate. It's even better if the activity involves some complex motor movements.

The optimal daily dose of exercise would be approximately 20 to 40 minutes in the morning.

Reduce Stress
Exercise increases concentrations of norepinephrine, a chemical that can moderate the brain's responses to stress.

Be More Productive
Research shows that workers who take time for exercise on a regular basis are more productive and have more energy than their more sedentary peers.

Boost happy Chemicals
Exercise releases endorphins, which create feelings of happiness and euphoria. Studies have shown that exercise can even alleviate symptoms among the clinically depressed.

Increase Relaxation
For some, a moderate workout can be the equivalent of a sleeping pill, even for people with insomnia.

Improve Self-Confidence
On a very basic level, physical fitness can boost self-esteem and improve positive self-image.

Sharpen Memory
Regular physical activity boosts memory and the ability to learn new things by increasing production of cells in the hippocampus responsible for memory and learning.

Exercise and Mental Health

Enjoy the Great Outdoors
Vitamin D acquired from soaking up the sun (while wearing sunscreen, of course!) can lessen the likelihood of experiencing depressive symptoms.

Boost Brainpower
Various studies have shown that cardiovascular exercise can create new brain cells (aka neurogenesis) and improve overall brain performance.

Alleviate Anxiety
The warm and fuzzy chemicals that are released during and after exercise can help people with anxiety disorders calm down.

Prevent Cognitive Decline
Diet and exercise can help shore up the brain against cognitive decline that begins after age 45. Working out, especially between age 25 and 45, boosts the chemicals in the brain that support and prevent degeneration of the hippocampus, an important part of the brain for memory and learning.

3: Minimize Caffeine Intake

Coffee drinkers everywhere are probably recoiling in horror at the very idea, but if you're serious about your efforts to change your brain for good, caffeine is something that is going to have to go. Or, at the very least, minimize the consumption you take in a day. This is because caffeine intake, especially if it is done in excess, can mimic the symptoms of anxiety which include an increased or accelerated heart rate, feelings of panic and anxiousness, and even feeling jittery. Caffeine can also impact your sleep cycle, and if you do not get enough sleep, your anxiety levels are going to remain on high alert which is going to make it much harder for you to overcome. After all, there's a reason why it's classified as a "drug."

It's easy to understand why we've become addicted to our morning cup of coffee. Next to oil, caffeine is the second most traded substance in the world. Most of us can't imagine starting the day without our regular Cup of Joe. it keeps us active, awake, and gives us that boost of energy we need to be on the go. But how exactly does coffee affect the brain? When we're awake, a chemical called *adenosine* accumulates slowing in the brain. This chemical is responsible for binding the receptors in the brain, slowing down its activity. As the day goes on, more adenosine is accumulated, and that's why we feel progressively tired as the day progresses. The more adenosine you have in the brain, the more tired you're going to feel. When we're asleep, our adenosine levels gradually decline, eventually leading to wakefulness once the mind and body have had enough rest.

Caffeine's structure is similar to that of adenosine, meaning when you consume caffeine, it competes and binds with the waiting adenosine receptors. However, since caffeine is *not* adenosine, you don't feel the effects of the sleepiness, thereby explaining why we feel alert and awake after those first few sips of warm liquid. But the downside is because you don't feel the effects of the sleepiness created by adenosine, the calming properties that are supposed to be brought on by sleepiness are not there either. With long-term use, your brain tries to compensate for this by creating more adenosine receptors, which in turn leads to more caffeine consumption to try and "stay awake." Caffeine is addictive and trying to quit is almost as hard as it is to try and quit smoking. Because caffeine impacts your brain's dopamine levels by stopping the reabsorption process, it makes you feel happy. The effects you get are similar to that of cocaine, except you're experiencing it to a lesser degree.

4: Being One with Nature

American biologist Edward O. Wilson in 1984 wrote about our deep primal need to affiliate with nature and the natural world and coined the term *biophilia hypothesis*. It is the idea that all of us have an innate tendency to seek out the connection we have with nature and other life forms. Wilson described it as a *"passionate love of life and everything that is alive,"* and he proposed that this affiliation we have with nature is part of our genetics. As we've become an even more urban species, biophilia is now more important than ever. More people today are living in cities than outside of it and the trend only continues to accelerate as people keep moving to big cities "where the jobs are." We have become an "indoor generation," and the average American today spends approximately 90% of their time indoors.

This radical shift in lifestyle has taken a toll on our minds and bodies. The physical side effects are easier to spot than the mental ones. Myopia, for example, which happens you don't get enough sunlight on your eyeballs, and they grow longer. Obesity, diabetes, cardiovascular diseases have all been linked to spending far too much time being sedentary indoors. To change our brains, we need to go back to nature and immerse ourselves in this multisensory therapy. Nature is full of wonders, from incredible sounds, tastes, textures, colors, shapes, and sizes. Being immersed in nature can be completely exhilarating and rejuvenating, and it is exactly what your overworked mind needs if you've been struggling to overcome negativity for a while now.

Rachel and Steven Kaplan from the University of Michigan put forth a prevailing theory about how spending time in nature can help us restore ourselves. Their theory is called the _Attention Restoration Theory_. They believe that by spending some time outdoors, like when watching the beautiful colors across the sky as the sun sets or gaze out at the serenity of the ocean, sitting at the park listening to the birds sing or going for a walk in the countryside is the much-needed therapy our brains need to reflect, rest, and restore ourselves. Even if you spent a few minutes every day looking out the window at the trees or a park, your mind is restoring itself, and that's the incredible power of what nature can do. As we go through life, our brain actually undergoes extraordinary development. It's the most adaptive organ in our body and it can change both positively and negatively by our thoughts, actions, and experiences. If you want to change your brain, feed it with positive experiences and spend more time outdoors disconnecting from the digital world.

5: The Power of Meditation

The incredible benefits of meditation are common knowledge. We've known for decades now that meditation can improve someone's physical and mental health, relieve stress, elevate mood, and even lower blood pressure levels. As more people are starting to realize its benefits on the brain, neuroscientists continue to study how meditation creates changes in brain structure and rewires our neural circuits by eliminating the connections we don't use that often while simultaneously strengthening the ones we do. By now, there's enough evidence to confidently suggest that the claims about the many benefits of meditation are no longer just flukes.

Studies that have been done suggest that meditation plays a role in contributing to the density of the hippocampus. This area of the brain is crucial for memory retention and tends to shrink as we age, but it turns out meditation can counteract those effects. Meditating for just 10 to 20 minutes a day is all you need to start restructuring and changing your brain. After several weeks of consistent meditation, you'll notice that you start to feel a lot calmer. You're more focused and calm under pressure, able to handle situations that would have ordinarily stressed you out. Both yoga and meditation are extremely effective for decreasing stress. They're particularly effective at reducing symptoms associated with numerous diseases, including depression, anxiety, pain, insomnia. With consistent practice, it can actually improve your ability to pay attention, and there's no shortage of studies that show people are happier and a lot more satisfied with their life when they regularly meditated.

Meditation is transformational. It doesn't just calm the mind; it changes who you are. Research participants who were put through an eight-week meditation-based *Stress Reduction Program* and told to meditate every day for 30 to 40 minutes experienced an enlargement in several areas of the brain; the hippocampus is one of them. What was even more interesting was how the change in gray matter was correlated with the change in stress. To experience the full benefits of all that meditation has to offer, you need to stick to it. It's not a one-off practice you only turn to when you need it. It's a *lifelong practice.*

When your body is overwhelmed by stress and anxiety, your brain begins flooding it with chemicals. These chemicals then activate the fight or flight response in your system, and those who struggle with anxiety remained in this heightened state of alertness and stress for a prolonged period. Our bodies are not meant to endure this, and it can quickly wear you down mentally and emotionally. Meditation has the opposite effect by inducing the relaxation response. The human mind has been referred to as the "monkey mind," with endless chattering and thoughts that are jumping around similar to a room full of monkeys. Meditation is the only way to learn how to manage them because the practice itself encourages mindfulness and awareness of every thought that takes place in the brain. Once you become the master of your thoughts, your brain becomes submissive and peaceful.

6: Getting Enough Sleep

It cannot be emphasized enough how important it is to get enough sleep at night. It's not just because you'll feel tired in the morning or grumpy throughout the day if you don't. A lack of sleep actually stops the brain from being able to initially make new memories. Imagine your brain was like an inbox. Without sleep, the memory in that inbox begins to shut down, making it impossible to remember anything, focus, or commit new experiences to memory. This means any new, incoming information is going to get bounced back because your brain can't absorb it anymore. It'll leave you feeling like an amnesic when you can't essentially make and create those new memories.

This is what happens to the sleep-deprived brain:

- You become emotional and on edge. When you're operating in a tired, burned-out mode running on little to no sleep, it doesn't take much for something to set you off. Difficulty sleeping can be attributed to worrying too much, and sleep deprivation can cause you to feel a lot more irritable than you normally would.

- When the brain doesn't get the sleep it needs, a toxic protein called the *beta-amyloid* is developed. This protein is associated with Alzheimer's disease, and without the proper deep sleep needed at night, the brain can't wash away the toxin and repair itself. The protein begins to build up and increase your risk of dementia in later life.

- Your reproductive system is affected. Men who only get 5-6 hours of sleep at night have the testosterone levels equivalent to someone who is 10 years older than they are.

- A lack of sleep could also act as a potential trigger for a short fuse. Have you ever noticed how things seem much harder or require more effort when you're feeling tired and fatigued from lack of sleep? You feel cranky, irritable, and even the smallest of things seem like a big deal. That is because your body is tired, your nerves are frayed, and a lack of sleep makes you less efficient than what you normally would be. It doesn't take much to set your temper off when you're sleep-deprived.

- Without proper sleep, you'll age a lot faster, and your immune system grows weaker, making it easier for you to fall prey to bacteria and viruses. There's a strong link between poor quality sleep and cancer that the World

Health Organization is now classifying working the night shift as potential carcinogens.

Your body and your brain need sleep to restore itself at night. Overcoming your brain and changing the way you think is not an easy task. It takes a lot of brainpower and energy, so it is important to give yourself a break whenever you need it.

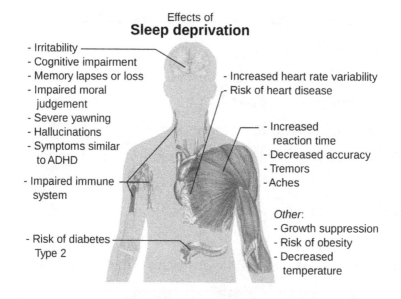

Effects of
Sleep deprivation

- Irritability
- Cognitive impairment
- Memory lapses or loss
- Impaired moral judgement
- Severe yawning
- Hallucinations
- Symptoms similar to ADHD
- Impaired immune system
- Risk of diabetes Type 2

- Increased heart rate variability
- Risk of heart disease

- Increased reaction time
- Decreased accuracy
- Tremors
- Aches

Other:
- Growth suppression
- Risk of obesity
- Decreased temperature

7: Regular Reading

Reading is almost like a lost art these days. After all, why read when you could easily watch a quick video summary of the book that highlights enough of the important key points you need. You get to save time this way, isn't that just as effective? Not exactly. The brain is like every other muscle and other than music, it needs reading to keep it stimulated. This is what happens to your brain when you read:

- Your focus improves
- You concentrate better
- Your mind absorbs the finer details of the story
- You forget your worries when you lose yourself in the story

Concentration is a big problem for a lot of people these days. Try spending half an hour away from your phone. Would you be able to do it? How long into that half an hour period will it be before your mind starts to think about how many notifications you've got or whether anyone tried to call you? On average, most people divide their time between their tasks. They check their emails while browsing social media. They chat with their colleagues while trying to finish an email. The biggest distraction of all? Our mobile phones.

When you read, you're transported to a different world. Even with a mind that is overworked and anxious. A 2009 study showed reading was the most effective way to overcome stress, beating out old favorites such as listening to music, enjoying a cup of tea or coffee, or even taking a walk, measured by evaluating heart rate and muscle tension. Participants in the study only took six minutes before their minds started to slow down and relax as soon as they began turning the pages of the book. Plus, everything you read is filling your head with new knowledge and information. The more well-read you are, the better equipped you will be to handle any challenges that come your way.

Reading is extremely beneficial for your brain, and it costs you nothing to do it. You already *know* this skill; all you need to do now is put it to good use and use it to change your brain and your perception. In 2013 there was a series of experiments. As done by two New York psychologists and David Kidd and Emmanuel Capstone. What they did was take people and ask them to requite short passages from various types of books. Some of them are nonfiction books explanatory or learning books. Some of them are sort of thrillers plots, where you really bad events happening in the story, but not very much about the people you weren't inside their heads. The third source was the sort of fiction which involves reading things from the perspective of the characters. As the researchers studied their brain activity, what they found was that those who struggled with relationships and social skills were the ones who were limited by their imagination. They simply did not have the ability to step outside themselves and had a difficult time imagining anything. Therefore, to create a shift in your mindset, you need to focus on reading material that encourages you to think outside the box.

8: Music for the Soul

Previously, it was thought that music was processed on the right side of the brain's hemisphere, but more recent research shows that music has the ability to affect all parts of our brain. It's interesting to see how some patients with brain damage couldn't retain their ability to read the contents of a newspaper *but somehow* remember how to read music. Or the way certain people lack the fine motor skills needed to do up the buttons of their sweater yet could play the piano with ease. Music has an almost healing, therapeutic effect on the brain, capable of altering our moods and our feelings. Music, in fact, stimulates the formation of certain chemicals in the brain. A perfect example to illustrate this point would be to observe the choice of music in movies. If you notice, it's not the scene that tells us how to feel; it's the *music*. With the right music in certain scenes, particularly the ones where the actors are not talking, the audience might be unclear about how they should feel or even understand what's going on. In a typical action or fight scene, it is the music that makes the scene epic, not so much the scene itself.

We tend to respond differently to happy and sad melodies. In one study that was conducted, it revealed that participants were more likely to interpret neutral expressions as sad expressions if the music they heard was sad. On the other hand, if it was happy music they heard, then they were more likely to perceive neutral expressions as happy instead. Dopamine is released in the brain when music is played, which is responsible for the satisfying feeling we get after listening to our favorite songs. Here's something interesting. When a person feels sad, they often find themselves listening to sad music, and surprisingly, that actually helps them feel better. Why? Because most of the time, when we feel sad or miserable, it's because we feel alone or misunderstood. Like no one understands us and we're all alone in the world. Listening to happy music, in this case, could end up making you feel worse because there's no attachment or anything that you can relate to. However, when you listen to sad music, your brain believes that the musician understands how you feel and being able to relate to the music helps to elevate your mood.

Listening to music, as it turns out, is similar to a full-body workout routine for your brain. However, given that our brains are as unique as our personalities, music does not affect everyone's brain in the same way. What one person enjoys might be someone else's idea of noise. Music that relaxes you and makes you feel happy could simultaneously make someone else feel bored. The best remedy for your brain would be to listen to the kind of music that works for you, particularly the ones that make you feel good. When you're stressed, overworked, anxious, depressed, or struggling with negativity, turning to your favorite playlist could be the shift in mindset that you need.

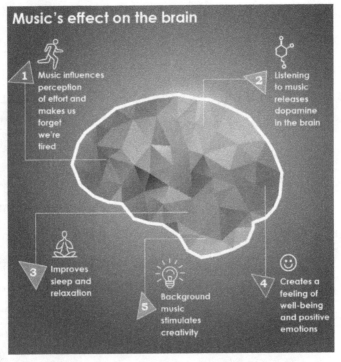

Image Source: <u>Polyclinique de l'Oreille</u>

9: Avoid Multitasking

Trying to do two (or several) things at once is the quickest way to ensure you're not doing anything well at all. Multitasking is not for everyone, and just because someone you know may be doing it, it doesn't necessarily mean it may be as effective for you as it is for them. Despite what society is trying to tell you, the human brain was not made for multitasking. When you try to handle more than a single task at a time, you either can't or won't do either task well. You *think* you're trying to save time, but really all you're doing is hampering your productivity.

Today, the expectation is you need to multi-task if you want to get several things done at once, but your poor, overworked brain needs enough time to focus on what it's doing, or you're going to feel mentally stuck. Unfortunately, the pressure of juggling multiple responsibilities has turned multitasking into an acceptable thing these days. There are numerous articles on the Internet that will try to convince you multitasking is a prized skill. Some employers even list it as part of the job requirements when interviewing new candidates. This false perception that multitasking is *acceptable* has only increased the amount of pressure and stress that is felt, keeping your brain in a prolonged fight or flight state of mind.

Truth be told, multitasking is ineffective in the long-run, and rather than promote better concentration; it promotes anxiety instead. When you're chasing the clock instead of focusing on what you're supposed to be doing, you get nervous, flustered and anxious when you notice you're running out of time. In the haste to meet the self- imposed time deadline you've set for yourself, your focus dissipates. Mistakes get made, crucial information gets overlooked, and you're feeling emotional from the pressure of rushing to meet your time goal so you can move onto your next task.

Our brains have a deliberate system, and while we may think we're handling tasks and completing them in a parallel manner, what the brain is actually doing is switching your attention back and forth between each activity. When you move from one task to the next, you can't pick up exactly where you left off. There's a reason for this. In 2009, a professor from the University of Minnesota, Sophie Leroy, introduced the concept of *attention residue*. When you move from A to B, your attention does not immediately do the same thing. While you're already getting started on B, your mind is still lingering on A, meaning that your attention is divided, and you're not as focused as you think you are.

Build a better mindset by knowing what works for you. If multitasking is just going to make you feel more overwhelmed than ever, then what you're doing is going to be counterproductive, instead of productive. Don't try to handle several things at once if this style of working isn't a good fit for you, focus on one thing at a time and get it done before moving onto the next if it's going to make you more productive.

10: A Grateful Heart and Mind

Oprah Winfrey once said: *"When you stop to look at what you have in your life, that is when you'll have more. If you only look at what you don't have, then you will never have enough."* Tony Robbins quoted something similar when he said: *"When you're grateful, that's when your fear disappears and abundance happens."* Gratitude is the attitude that brings success. day. Gratitude is one of the healthiest positive emotions that we can feel as a person. If you observed how those who are always grateful every day somehow seem like they are more resilient to stress, that's an example of how powerful a grateful heart and mind can be.

Out of all the 10 steps talked about in this chapter, this is by far the *easiest* to begin implementing immediately. The effects are instantaneous too. Not only does gratitude actively remind you of the things you have to be grateful for, but when you actively remind yourself of all the good experiences you have in your life, it eventually helps to magnify positive thoughts and soon, the positive thoughts will eventually be strong enough to overpower the negative and toxic emotions. Studies have been done on the subject of gratitude, and it has proven that this is an immensely powerful tool in developing a sense of happiness and wellbeing. It's hard to remain pessimistic when you think about all the blessings you have in your life. If you woke up this morning and you can think about more than one thing that you are grateful for, then you are a very blessed person and it's time to remind yourself of that every day.

Chapter 4: How Do I Get Smarter?

Is it possible that we could get smarter? Does knowledge itself make you a smarter person? What about all those brain-teasing puzzles and games? Do they actually do anything to improve your cognitive abilities? Let's explore the idea of intelligence and the way that it is defined and measured. How much do we know about makes one brain intelligent if compared to another? No structure of biochemistry exists that can pinpoint exactly and say for certain *this is what makes someone smart.* The brain is made up of billions of cells, and as we know, different areas of the brain are responsible for different functions. A lot going on inside your brain.

Keeping Your Brain in Peak Condition

Increasing your focus, mental clarity, concentration, memory power. We want to do all of this, but the question is *how?* How do we keep our brains in peak condition, so we become strategic, logical, analytical thinkers who are primed for success in both our personal and professional lives? A strategic mindset helps you stay on the path to success, a skill that is going to be particularly useful when you're working in a demanding and volatile career. One minute you may have to make decisions on-the-fly, and other times you need to maintain a rational and level head. Strategic thinking is how you keep yourself prepared and ready to respond the way that you need to. Even if you're not a successful entrepreneur or business person, strategic thinking is a skill set that is going to serve you well in your job and perhaps other facets of your life where you might need it.

Strategic, logical thinkers have an advantage over everyone else. Not only are they smarter and more analytical, they know how to maximize their strengths and efficiency, using them as leverage to help them get one step ahead of everyone else. Training their brains to think like a strategist has allowed them to plan what the next logical steps are and figure out what the most direct route to success is going to be. The added benefit of training your brain to think smarter is you learn to develop problem-solving skills. These skills make you think about approaching one problem from multiple avenues with the goal of applying the most productive, effective, and logical approach to resolve the problem. You'll learn how to comprehend the problem at stake and this, in turn, gives you a deeper understanding of their personal and professional goals.

Smart thinkers don't take anything for granted. They consider every option, every possibility, and every avenue carefully before making a move. They question, they analyze, they evaluate, and they don't limit themselves to a rigid way of responding to maximize their effectiveness. They think outside the box and come up with solutions no one else might have even considered, thanks to this skill. By learning how to think smarter, the ideas that you are going to bring to the table are going to be innovative and fresh, and often yield better results than what the traditional approach might have brought. Developing this skill will allow you to focus on developing and sourcing new and better opportunities while challenging the normal assumptions, and the solutions you come up with will hold greater value, thanks to your ability to think creatively outside the box.

Now, there are six mental strategies that can put you on the path to thinking smarter, but before you can do that, you need to understand something about the human brain. To become smart thinking strategist we want to be, we need to learn how to engage the *entire* brain in the process. The brain is all about making connections, and to think smarter, there are two types of thinking you need to tap into:

- **Divergent Thinking** - Observing the bigger picture and then work on generating ideas.

- **Convergent Thinking** - Examining and rearranging these ideas in a rational manner.

Both of these types of thinking can be cultivated through regular brain training exercises and the mental strategies which will be covered below. Studies claim the most innovative type of thinkers is the ones who can quickly switch between these two thinking styles. To make that quick transition, you need to use your entire brain and make conscious decisions to alternate from one style of thinking to the next. The *Six Thinking Hats* technique was pioneered by Edward De Bono, and it is a technique that capitalizes on this ability. De Bono's approach was to confront the problem using "six different hats" and reflect using the divergent and convergent thinking. In other words, you need to be an active participant in the thinking process to use your entire brain.

Image Source: We are IVE

Mental Strategy 1: Read Every Day

American entrepreneur Jim Rohn once said: *"You are the average of the five people that you surround yourself with."* There is a lot of truth to this statement. If you look at the five people you're closest to right now, how would you describe them? Are they successful? Do they prefer to take it easy and sail through life hoping for the best? Are they ambitious or complacent? Committed or unreliable? If they happen to be people who don't exactly have specific goals, dreams or a purpose they are working toward, chances are you're probably on the same level as they are. But if your closest companions are ambitious, driven, and motivated, there's a good chance you're just like them too. There are a lot of factors that influence who we are as human beings. Our environment is one of them. We copy each other and we excel at this trait, which is how slangs, accents, traditions, and cultures came about. People who spend enough time together start adopting each other's habits and mindsets.

It comes as no surprise then that a lot of successful individuals have attributed a lot of their success to their mentors. People whom they learned from and emulated. Mark Zuckerberg looked up to Steve Jobs. Martin Luther King found a wonderful mentor in Gandhi. Bill Gates learned a lot from his time with Warren Buffet. One of the few things successful people have in common is that they always have at least one person in their social sphere who is *already* a success. These are the people they learned from, whose habits and mindsets they adopted. Now, you might be thinking, *"I don't have anyone successful in my life. I can spend a lot of time with and learn from,"* but you would be wrong about that. You *have books.*

A book is your gateway into the mindsets of the successful and the wealthy. It is packed with ideas, strategies, tips, suggestions, advice based on firsthand experience. Successful people have taken all their knowledge and packaged it into a convenient, easy to carry a book that you can bring with you anywhere you go. Any time you need a burst of inspiration, pick up the book and immerse yourself in their world. It is as good as having the person there speaking directly to you. At least 75% of self-made millionaires reportedly make it a point to read at least two books a month.

Reading books is the most obvious way to enrich your vocabulary and, simultaneously, your intelligence. It is the easiest way you get to pick and choose *who* you want to learn from and whose ideas and words of wisdom are going to influence you the most. Every bit of information you read is going to shape your mindset and perception. This is the easiest self-development tool that you can use to your benefit.

Mental Strategy 2: Brain Games

Brain games are a popular way of challenging your mind. From Sudoku, scrabble, crossword puzzles, math's problems, and more, nothing fills you with a sense of triumph, quite like solving a particularly hard crossword or Sudoku puzzle with no help. These complex puzzles are brain food that fuels your ability to think logically as you scan your brain trying to figure out the answers with the small set of clues you've been given in the crossword puzzle. Sudoku puzzles encourage you to harness your analytical and mathematical thinking abilities. Combine these skills together and you're well on your way to becoming a logical master. These activities stimulate thinking and activities like these are an enjoyable way to improve your brainpower.

One game has managed to withstand the test of time. This same game has survived for so long because it has been shown to stimulate more cognitive improvement than any other. That game is *chess,* and it's been around for nearly 1500 years. People around the world have, at one time or another, tried their hand at this complex mind game. For a long time, this game was exclusively played only by royalty or other members of high society. A game where two opponents manipulate a set of 16 pieces to try and outthink and outmaneuver their opponent. The game grew in popularity because of its strategic diversity and intricacy. It keeps the brain sharp by forcing you to think several steps ahead and plan your moves if you're going to win. To checkmate your opponent, you'll have to apply creative thinking to seemingly complex problems.

Here's how chess affects your brain. You'll need to rely on your short-term memory to quickly process the moves your opponent makes. You'll then need to tap into your long-term memory regurgitate any effective strategies already stored in your memory bank to plan your counter-attack. Next, you rely on your spacial and visual abilities to recognize openings to make your move. Therefore, you're engaging several areas of the brain through one seemingly simple game. Both planning and creative thinking are needed for strategic adaptation, and chess clearly requires quite a bit of mental gymnastics on your part. When you're playing in a professional capacity, all of that thinking above needs to be done within a certain time limit, which means your brain needs to be constantly on top of its game, consistently focused and alert. If it doesn't, you won't be thinking as clearly and that might give your opponent the upper hand when you're not performing at your best. The cognitive intensity that is demanded from this game can put quite a bit of stress on the brain, but like physical exercise, a little stress can be good for you. You might say it is even necessary since it is important to occasionally challenge the brain and push it beyond its comfort zone, just like you would with any other physical muscle in your body. A fit brain continues performing at its best even as we grow older.

One study discovered that students who were immersed in a chess program experienced a dramatic improvement in their reading abilities. Another study revealed that when chess was immersed in a high school math's curriculum, students experienced an increase in their problem-solving abilities and raised test scores too. Intelligence may be a broad concept, but it is evident that this particular mind game is going to benefit you cognitively across the board.

Mental Strategy 3: Get Regular Exercise

The typical stereotype scenario pits brains against brawn. However, this stereotype couldn't be further from the truth. Athleticism and intelligence are partners, not opponents. When you're good at one, you naturally begin improving at the other. The mind is not the only thing that needs exercise. The Harvard Health Letter is one study that believes exercises can do you a world of good in terms of improving your thinking and memory power. Exercise, according to this study, helps to stimulate the release of growth factors and chemicals in the brain that impacts the growth of new blood vessels and how healthy our brain cells are. The healthier your brain cells, the better you become at logical thinking and reasoning.

Your body is controlled and motivated by your mind. Exercise is the healthiest and most natural way to give your brain the energy boost it needs. All it takes is a 15-minute workout to increase your motivation and keep your mind sharp enough to think clearly throughout the rest of your day. With that added boost of concentration, you're able to learn and digest information a lot more easily. Since exercise releases endorphins that make you feel happy and healthy, this burst of enthusiasm makes it easier for your brain to retain information. Have you ever tried taking a test or solving a problem while you were in a bad mood? How did it go? Not very well, obviously. That's because strong emotions like sadness and anger can cloud your judgment and hinder your critical thinking abilities.

Exercise also stimulates the *neurogenesis* process. During this process, your brain grows new neurons. As we age, the population of neurons in the brain begins to decrease, but exercise can counter the aging process by helping the brain regenerate neurons. The new growth lowers the risks of anxiety and depression, commonly associated with *neural atrophy*.

Mental Strategy 4: Learning A New Language

Language happens to be one of the most sophisticated things that your brain can do. Each time you speak, several areas of the brain begin working in tandem to formulate words, structure sentences, and construct meaning. What a lot of us don't realize is exactly how big of a role the brain plays in our linguistics development. Since we can't see or feel our brains working when we're speaking, it doesn't seem like the brain is doing a lot. Although it seems like the larynx is hard at work creating the sounds and our tongue and lips work just as hard to manipulate those sounds and turn them into words, it is the *brain* that controls them all. Without the brain, the larynx, throat, and tongue would be pretty useless. Without instructions coming from the brain, no one would be able to understand what you're trying to say.

There are two neurological deficiencies that happen in the brain in relation to language, called *Broca's Aphasia* and *Wernicke's Aphasia*. The word *aphasia*, in general, happens when your language production is impaired due to damage inflicted on the brain.

- **Broca's Aphasia** - Affects the *Broca's area,* a major region of language production. This area of the brain is mainly responsible for creating complex speech. Deficiencies in this area could lead to difficulties forming sentences and difficult grammar. Speech often sounds simple and slow because this part of the brain can't function the way that it should. Those who struggle with Broca's Aphasia often experience frustration as they struggle to communicate. They know in their minds what they want to say, but their brain still struggles to translate that fluid message into words.

- **Wernicke's Aphasia** - This area of the brain is responsible for helping you create meaningful speech, which means damage inflicted to this area could cause your words to lose meaning entirely. Those who struggle with this condition can get the words out of their mouths, but they struggle to connect those words in an organized way. Their sentences could end up sounding like a jumble of unrelated ideas. Unlike those dealing with Broca's Aphasia, Wernicke's Aphasia individuals sometimes don't realize that something is wrong. To them, the words are coming out just like they are supposed to, not realizing that they are nearly impossible to understand.

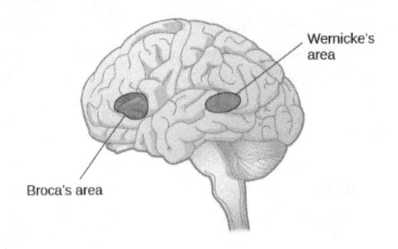

Image Source: <u>Lumen Learning</u>

As you can see, even if your voice, mouth, and tongue are working perfectly, language is still a process that is deeply neurological. This means each time you practice language, you're exercising your brain more than you think. When you listen, write, read, or speak, your brain is making several new connections and overcoming challenges and creating new ideas all at once. A <u>study</u> conducted in 2012 in Sweden examined a group of young adults who started studying a foreign language. Each student participant in this study only spoke one language when they first began. Over the course of three months, these students were given daily courses in either Russian, Arabic, or Dari. Each student's brain was scanned before and after the study to detect if learning a new language would cause the brain to grow. The researchers also wanted to determine that any brain growth experienced during this experiment was a product of learning a new language, and not just learning in general.

At the end of the three-month stint, the brain scans of these students were compared to the scans of regular cognitive science students. Both groups of students had to spend the same amount of time in class and an equal amount of time studying. The only difference is the group of cognitive science students was not focused on learning a new language alone. Interesting enough, by the end of the experiment, it was the group learning a new language that showed an expansion in their brains. This development correlated with their language proficiency. In other words, the linguistics students showed the most neurological growth out of the two groups tested. When the results were compared against the cognitive group, the difference was even more obvious. The students who learned a second language were the ones who showed significant development over the other group.

General learning improves intelligence, but learning a second language (or even a third or fourth) engages several diverse areas, and being multilingual is among the best ways to keep the brain in peak condition. It's a good thing that learning a new language these days is easier than ever, thanks to technology.

Mental Strategy 5: Manage Your Time Wisely

Time is all that we have. Ancient philosophers were intrigued by this one, simple question: *How do we use our time in a way that makes our lives a lot more meaningful?* That's a very good question. Are you spending your time as efficiently as you should be? How do you manage, organize, and plan your time in a day so you can get all the tasks that you need to do done? If you are given 8 hours a day at work, it is up to you to divide your time and allocate your tasks accordingly to everything gets done within those 8 hours, and you do this by allocating the right amount of time to the tasks at hand based on priority. If time is such a limited resource, how do we know if we're making the *smartest* use of our time? How do we make sure that every minute we invest in something is a minute that is well spent? Because once that minute is gone, it's gone forever. Nothing you can do is going to bring it back.

The modern-day concept of time management is about tips and tricks on how to get more done. How to be more productive, how to do things faster, how to work better, and how to be more efficient. Roman Stoic philosopher Seneca said this: *"If we value our time as money, then we are valuing our time very cheaply."* Why do we do this? Because we think we've got a lot of time. Changing your brain and improving yourself involves learning how to manage your time better so you are living your most productive life. Time is a precious commodity, one that we don't have a lot of. If you use the time you have been given wisely, you are going to succeed in all the different facets of your life. A productive person can accomplish several things in a day. An average person accomplishes the bare minimum at best in a day. These two people are given the exact same 24-hours in a day, yet the difference between the one who succeeds and the one who is just getting by is how well they manage their time.

Neuroplasticity tells us that it is possible to rewire the brain for success. What happens in our brain is based on what activities we spend the most time on. Every time you practice something, like the piano or playing a sport, you know that you get better with each practice. That's because the area of the brain that is involved is expanding, and when it does, you get better at what you're doing. The thing is, your brain's capacity is not an unlimited resource. There is only so much capacity in the brain allocated for activities, so it is up to you to decide which activities should be prioritized. You must decide which activities are important to you and that's where time management comes in. Effective time management is going to involve several different aspects of your day, among which could include setting goals, planning tasks and preparing a to-do list to keep you organized, delegating responsibilities, setting your priorities and determining how much time to allocate to the tasks you have based on importance. If your routine prior to this was to just wake up in the morning and go with the flow or a general idea of what needs to be done which you made a mental note of, this is about to change. All it requires is a small tweak in your routine to bring about big changes in your productivity.

Most of us have lost the ability to concentrate thanks to social media, and the average attention span now spans between 7-minutes. It has become so easy to get distracted these days it's hard to recall the last time you were able to walk into your office and devote an entire day to focusing on your tasks without interruptions or distractions. Imagine how much more you could get done in a day if you weren't distracted at all? Time management comes down to *attention*. The difference between success and failure is sometimes down to how well you can *train your brain to pay attention*. Often, the ones who achieve the most are those who have mastered the art of time management, using it to their advantage, *and focusing on the task without allowing themselves to get distracted*. It's not about how much time you have, but rather *how well you use the time you have been given*. With proper time management, you will notice a world of difference in the way that your life is run.

For every action, there is a consequence. This adage is especially true with time management. Each time you procrastinate and put a task off, it is going to have consequences. Often, you'll end up falling behind; you might miss an opportunity, you might get swamped with even more tasks later on and find it even more difficult to manage time. That's not smart. Time is its own master, and while you may not be able to manage or control it, you can certainly control *what you do* with your own time. *That's the smart thing to do.* If you want to be a different person tomorrow than you are today, you have to be attentive to the things you want to focus on. If you say you want to get better at giving speeches, then you need to practice it day after day until the synapses and connections in your brain are reinforced. Right now, the smart thing for you to do would be to *choose* the synapses and connections in your brain you want to reinforce. Persist and keep practicing until there is visible change happening in your life *because your brain has changed.* Author Winifred Gallager said: *"You are the sum total of what you are focusing on."* This quote points out how our reality is dictated by what we pay attention to and it is dictated by how you are spending your time. If you want your life to matter, you need to start focusing on the things that matter and dedicate more time to those areas because these are the areas that make you the happiest.

Mental Strategy 6: Review Learned Information

Here's another problem that comes with living in a distracted world. The inability to focus means we have difficulty retaining the information we absorb sometimes. Memory can be a fickle thing, even more so with the distractions we face that threaten to disrupt our concentration. Distractions are everywhere, and sometimes it can be hard to remember something you've just read even if you only read it 5-minutes ago. Other times, when you're not even trying, you'll come across and odd random fact or two that you'll remember forever. It's funny how our memory works. Unless something resonates with you so strongly that it leaves a memorable impression right away, chances are you don't retain a lot of the information that you're exposed to every day. But if we don't retain the information long enough to review what we've learned, *how do we get smarter then?*

Studies about human memory date back as far as 2,000 years, and even today, new discoveries about how memory works continue to get made. The downside to living in the information age is that there's too much information. It is literally information overload, and it becomes hard to distinguish fact from fiction, especially on the internet. Information overload is not doing your brain or your memory any favors. As we've just learned from the point above, our brain has a finite capacity. There's only so much it can take it at any given time and when the brain is overloaded, it eventually leads to mental blocks and sometimes a complete shutdown altogether. We only become acutely aware of our memories when we realize we've forgotten something. This presents a huge problem when you're trying to recall information that you've read. Reading for comprehension becomes a challenge when you struggle to retain the text. In 2016, three British scientists were winners of the largest neuroscience prize in the world worth a staggering 1 million Euros for the work they did related to human memory. What Bliss, Morris, and Collingridge discovered was that in both memory loss and memory formation, there was a protein in the brain that holds the key, but there's still a lot to be understood and discovered.

To understand how we're going to improve our memory power enough to retain the information we have learned, we first need to understand how the brain works in this capacity. Essentially, the brain process memory in three staged:

- The encoding stage
- The storage stage
- The recall stage

The encoding stage happens each time your brain is presented with a new piece of information or notices something new. It starts to consciously perceive the images, sound, and all the other sensory details. For example, when you take a holiday to a new destination. Your memory of that place is formed by your visual, auditory system, and other senses. Visuals, as you take in the beauty and wonder of your surroundings. Auditory, as you notice the hum of traffic out on the busy street. Other senses like smell when you get a whiff of the wonderful street food scents that come your way. Every time you think about this location even long after you've left your holiday behind, the memory is still as strong.

The storage stage is when all this new information that you gathered is moved to the storage part of your brain. Your memories are stored in several areas of the brain, not just in a single area alone. The brain's neurons then "talk" to each other by passing signals across. When this happens, the neurons are building either long-lasting or temporary connections, and the strength of those connections helps you retain your memories. Short-term memory stores information in your brain temporarily, before either dismissing it or transferring the information into long-term memory storage. Do you remember what you had for lunch two weeks ago? Probably not, since once the meal has been devoured, the brain can finally let go of that information. Long-term memories, on the other hand, are what you can hold onto for months, weeks, and a lifetime. Like the first time, you rode your bike. Both long and short-term memories do get weaker with age because of how our brain cells lose the connections that happen between the neurons over time. Exercising your memory enough, though, can prevent this from happening.

The recall stage is the final stage of the brain's entire memory processing system. When you need to replay or retrieve a piece of memory from your brain, that's the recall process at work. To do this, the brain needs to revisit the old nerve pathways responsible for creating that memory in the first place. When you repeatedly recall those memories, the brain's connection strengthens, and one example of this is when students repeatedly go through their notes before a big exam, so the information stays "fresh" in their minds. Recalling memories are not always accurate, though. Sometimes certain memories can get mixed up with another, which explains the false memory phenomenon.

So, how do we change our brain and boost our memory and powers of concentration to become smarter? By *keeping the mind and body healthy*. Enhancing your memory prowess goes beyond just techniques and strategies alone. It comes down to the way you live and the quality of your health that also plays a vital role in your overall mental and brain health too. The healthier you are, the healthier your brain is. Better sleep, better nutrition, regular exercise, and healthier lifestyle choices make a difference. If you needed any proof of this, all you would need to do is go out and have a big, fast food meal and then try to concentrate after you're done eating. Not an easy thing to do when you're feeling sluggish and tired from excess sodium and all sorts of other unhealthy ingredients you know are not good for your body.

Chapter 5: Breaking Free of Bad Habits

We know procrastination is not good. We know eating fast food is not good. We know spending hours aimlessly browsing social media is a waste of precious time. We know smoking is terrible for our health. We know these and several other bad habits are not doing us any favors. So why is it so hard to resist temptation? Why do we keep doing them, even though we know we're going to regret it later? No good can come of it, but somehow, we can't seem to stop ourselves from continually committing these bad habits. The temptation to give in has an immense pull, and it's not easy training your mind to stay on task for a sustained period. What makes it even harder is we were never taught the proper methods to maintain focus. When it comes to focusing your mind, most of us are left to our own devices to try and figure it out on our own. Add these bad habits into the mix and it is no wonder we struggle to stay on track and stay productive.

What Are Bad Habits and Why Do They Affect Us?

Logically, we should be avoiding bad habits if they don't align with our goals and keep hampering the results we want to get. There's a simple explanation for this, and it goes back to the way we were evolved. Humans did not evolve with a preference for delayed gratification. We evolved to prioritize immediate gratification. We want actions that are going to yield the most benefit in the current moment. That's because our ancestors relied on this mechanism to survive when they had to hunt for food and secure shelter. Since our very survival depended on it, at the time, it made sense to place a higher value on the actions that were going to bring immediate benefit. For our ancestors, the possibility of what might happen in the future was not such a pressing concern. When our ancestors found food, they ate it immediately instead of waiting until tomorrow, since tomorrow was not a guarantee.

Fast forward to today's modern society, where we no longer have to spend our days hunting for food for running away from predators. The environment we live in now is all about delayed gratification. Save money now and enjoy it when you retire. Diet and exercise now and reap the rewards in the future. Plan your finances wisely now and buy the house you want several years down the road. Do a good job today and you'll receive your paycheck in a few weeks. We work for years and invest the necessary time and effort needed before we start to see any results for the hard work, we put in. Yes, the rewards in the modern world are all about delayed gratification. *But* our human nature remains the same, and that's the problem. Our brains are still wired to prioritize instant gratification, which makes the allure of bad habits hard to resist.

How Habits Are Formed

Our brain is a powerful organ that learns your habits-whether or not you are trying to teach it. You might have noticed that the mind has a tendency to easily absorb the negative influences and bad habits faster than it does with positive, nurturing habits that require substantially more work. The formation of habit begins with two traits you must adopt if this is going to work:

- Self-discipline
- Willpower.

To most people, self-discipline feels constricting, but in reality, when you practice it, you began to that your life before you were disciplined was constricting. You realize that how you spend your time, the bad habits you had, and the addictions were controlling your life all this while. But when you are self-disciplined, you are more in control and you have more say of how you live your life. Your words will become actions and your actions will become habits. Your habits shape your characters and your character becomes your destiny. Practicing self-discipline is a short-term pain that comes with numerous benefits in the long run.

With bad habits, the rewards you get are immediate, but the consequences come later. Smoking will kill you in the future, but in the current moment, it feels good. Procrastinating work in favor of binge-watching your favorite shows makes you feel happy now, but the stress of rushing to meet deadlines at the last minute will eventually catch up to you. To the human brain, any reward we get right away seems more valuable than a future reward which is not a guarantee. an ingrained pattern of behavior. Once a habit has become so deeply rooted and ingrained in you, it becomes even more difficult to break out of.

Bad habits may seem destructive, but that's not how they were meant to be. We indulge in these bad habits because we get a sudden urge or craving for them. Our brains did not evolve with a strong desire to check social media every 10 minutes. It didn't evolve with the urge to keep eating fast food every day or smoke several cigarettes throughout the day. We certainly did not involve to want to spend hours on the couch watching one episode after another. All those cravings came about because of an underlying motive. On a deeper level, people might smoke or drink as a way of self-medicating to relieve themselves from anxiety or depression. Maybe they turn to social media because they want to feel accepted or feel a connection to someone else. Maybe watching one episode after another and spending hours in front of Netflix helps them feel relaxed after a long and stressful day. In other words, the habits we have today are nothing more than modern-day solutions that we have come up with to help us cope with the pressure and expectations that we may be faced with. We give in to them because they make us feel good or serve some benefit.

Since the delayed consequences of many of these bad habits are so far in the future, the realization doesn't hit us about how bad these habits are until it's actually happening. A bad habit is defined as any habit that stands in the way of you achieving your long-term goals. These bad habits tend to stick around for two reasons. The first is because they are ingrained in us, and the second is because they almost always lead to short-term goals. Logically, you know your long-term goals are more important. But it's difficult to remind your brain of that. To break out of these mental bad habits, you need a reason that is well-defined, clear and compelling enough. There's another problem though. Some of these bad habits are satisfying a need that we have, and cutting out these bad habits completely means that we are going to be left with certain needs that are unmet. Simplistic advice about just quitting bad habits is never going to work effectively in the long-term. Maybe you'll stop them for a while, but once the craving or need for it gets too much, you'll find yourself slipping back into your old ways in no time.

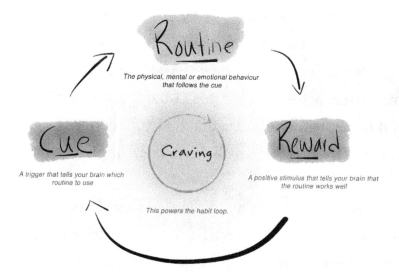

Image Source: <u>The Mindful Company</u>

Is It Possible to Change These Habits?

Bad habits will cost you your happiness, so why indulge in them any longer than you have to? Once you understand why these bad habits happen, yes, it is possible to change these bad habits. In one of his many private journals, renowned martial artist Bruce Lee once said: *"I realize that my mind's dominating thoughts will eventually reproduce in outwards, physical action that will gradually transform and become my physical reality. Therefore, I will choose to concentrate my thoughts daily for 30 minutes. I will think about the person I intend to become and create a clear mental picture in my mind."* What we can learn from Lee is we need a reason that is compelling enough to change the way we think when it comes to bad habits, and it begins with the realization that your current bad habits may not be the best way to solve the underlying issues you face.

Bad habits are nothing more than a method you picked up along the way to cope with certain issues, and the good news is, there is always more than one solution to every problem. One person learns to cope with the stress they feel by smoking, while another may learn to cope by exercising. The same problem, but the latter solution is a much better option. Breaking out of bad habits is tough because of the constant craving to give in to temptation. Therefore, what you need to do is find a similar replacement that is going to give you that same kind of reward.

This will encourage the shift toward a habit that is more productive, eventually getting rid of the bad habit you've been carrying around gradually. It's going to require some digging into your thoughts to find what the actual reward is that you crave. If you're repeatedly engaging in a habit knowing that it is bad for you anyway, there must be a reason why. Once you find that reason, think about something similar (but better) that could give you the same benefits.

Your Habit Replacement Journey

Eliminate your bad habits by sticking to a new way of thinking. It starts with a three-step process:

- **Step 1** - First, you need to make a list of all the bad habits that are holding you back.

- **Step 2** - Once you've done that, identify the triggers that are causing your habitual bad behavior.

- **Step 3** - Find healthier, better replacements for those habits that give you the same good feeling.

For example, if you list one of your bad habits as spending too much time aimlessly browsing through social media and you've identified the trigger as boredom, the next step is to think about a suitable replacement. When you're bored, why not try reading instead? You still have the same cravings you did before, except now you're trying to replace it with a better solution that is more aligned with your goals.

Now, this three-step process may sound simple enough, but there's more to it than that. Because these habits have been going on for a while now, you might still find yourself unconsciously performing these bad habits *even* when you know there's an alternative solution. When you catch yourself doing this, that means you need to take it one step further by optimizing your environment to minimize the temptation you feel. The environment we're in has a big impact on our behavior. If the things that encourage your bad habits are always easily accessible and in a visible place, you're going to find yourself reaching for them without thinking about it. In the example above, you would optimize your environment by keeping a book next to you while putting your phone in a drawer or tucked away somewhere else where you're not tempted to pick it up every few minutes. You could also opt to delete your social media apps from your phone and install them with apps that motivate you to read instead. You'll still be able to access social media from your laptop, but the temptation won't be as strong because it's not as easily accessible as your phone. The aim is to add as many "hurdles" as possible that make it harder to reach your bad habits, so you're less likely to do them. By manipulating your surroundings so it works in your favor, you can dramatically increase your chances of successfully changing your habits.

To boost your chances of success, even more, you need to motivate yourself. Your new replacement habits might not feel as satisfying as the old ones. Not yet at least. To motivate yourself, you need a reward system in place that gives you something to look forward to. For example, if you make it through an entire day reaching for your book instead of your phone each time you were bored, you can reward yourself with 30-minutes of social media time at the end of the day once all your tasks have been completed. This positive reinforcement trains you to be disciplined enough to stick to the commitment you've made so the reward at the end of the day feels even more satisfying because you know that you've earned it. Another way to go the extra mile making sure you succeed at your attempts to change your habits is by making yourself accountable. Tracking your progress is the best way to do this. Each time you successfully stick to your new habits, mark the day on your calendar. Add an extra layer of challenge by trying to stick to your new habit each day so you're consistently checking off days on your calendar. The visual progress you see happening on your calendar will motivate you to keep going and not break the success streak you see.

Tracking your progress is the best way to feel motivated. When you can see yourself moving forward, you're motivated to keep going down the right path when you see how far you've come already. Breaking bad habits requires perseverance. The longer you've been living with the bad habit you're trying to change, the longer it's going to take to break out of that cycle, and you need that perseverance to keep you going. The only way you can really fail is by giving up.

Shift Your Mindset to Break Your Habits

It's okay to make mistakes along the way when you're trying to get better. When we make a mistake, we immediately start to feel defeated and be too hard on ourselves. That's not how things are supposed to be. You're supposed to make mistakes because it's part of the learning process. When you start seeing your mistakes as part of the learning process, you open your mind to undergoing that learning process. You stop being too hard on yourself, and you feel significantly less stressed when you take away the pressure of trying to get it perfect right away. A shift in your mindset requires focus. To focus on *why you're working this hard* to change your break and break free of your old ways.

These guidelines might help you get started:

- **Think About Your Loved Ones** - Loved ones can be an immensely powerful and motivating factor to bring about the change you need. What do you want your legacy to be? What do you want to leave behind for your family? Do you want them to remember you as someone who was stressed all the time? Someone who had difficulty coping? Would you want your children or other members of your family picking up on the negative habits you have? What better reason to change for the better than to do it for the people you love?

- **Don't Disregard Your Feelings** - Some bad habits are triggered by our emotions. When we're uncomfortable with the emotions we feel, we try to find an escape route of some sort. For example, you're uncomfortable feeling alone and isolated, so you turn to social media for some kind of solace or comfort. The negative, self-deprecating thoughts you have about yourself happen when you're uncomfortable with the emotions you feel. When you feel terrible about yourself, you start binging on unhealthy food, and you lose all desire to accomplish anything because you think, *"What's the point?"*. Emotions are uncomfortable, and you wouldn't be the first person who finds themselves going to great lengths to try and avoid that discomfort. You probably even try to escape those feelings by indulging in bad mental habits like feeling sorry for yourself or adopting the victim mentality. The only way to deal with your uncomfortable emotions is to go through them. To be comfortable enough to let them in, experience them, and then move forward.

- **Saying "NO" Is Not Wrong** - You might not like it, but you have to do it. You owe it to yourself to manage your stress levels, so you don't keep turning back to your bad habits as a way to make yourself feel better. The cycle needs to be broken and one way to do it is by learning to say no when you need to. There will be some moments in life when you need to say no. Even if you feel guilty doing it. When you know it's the right thing to do in the long run, then you must be willing to do what needs to be done. If you've already got too many things to focus on your plate right now, know when it is time to decline a request and you don't have to feel guilty about it. The tasks that you have on hand right now should be given attention and priority until they have been completed. Remember the human brain is not designed for multitasking. If you want to excel at anything, you must learn to focus on one thing at a time. Unless something is extremely urgent, if you already have your hands full, then learn to say no.

- **Scheduling "Think Time"** - It is always better to be well-prepared than to just wing it or go with the flow. If you find that leaving things to chance tends to elevate your stress levels, plan ahead as much as you can, and take comfort in the knowledge that you're as prepared as you can be. The more organized you are, the less likely you're going to be to get easily distracted by your bad habits. You don't even have to go too far, by planning a week ahead of a month, maybe even a year ahead. Keep it simple by keeping it focused on planning for the next day. Scheduling "think time" is a crucial way to prepare yourself and to stay on track because you have a goal that you're working toward. When you've got a lot of your task list to get through, planning your time wisely is an effective stress management approach. The less stressed you are, the less need there will be to go searching for your old bad habits make yourself feel better. It's a good idea to ensure you give yourself some "buffer time" in between tasks too. Handling one task after another in a row with no break time is a one-way destination to burning out quickly. As much as you would quickly like to go through your task list and get everything done and over with as soon as possible, it is still important to give yourself time to recharge between each task by taking the needed breaks. When scheduling your tasks for the day, it is important that you leave some buffer time in between to allow yourself to recharge your mental energy. Buffer time also gives you some time to think about how you're doing and if there's anything that could be done better.

Thought Replacement

One bad habit that needs to be broken is allowing negative thoughts to stop us in our tracks. Instead of using mistakes as a lesson and a motivation to propel us forward to keep getting better, the habit of thinking negative uses mistakes as a weapon to beat us down even more. A lot of thoughts happen without us being aware of it, and these thoughts either inspire or reprimand us. Negative thoughts, unfortunately, happen to be the stronger force, and unless you practice thought replacement, they can quickly overpower any attempt at staying positive. Overcoming negativity for good is probably going to be one of the hardest challenges you might have faced in a while. Breaking out of old habits that have been around for years is never an easy or straightforward process. It takes weeks of exercising positive thought replacement, which is where you replace your bad thoughts with good ones. It will take a while before you begin to feel the visible shift from a heavy, cluttered, disorganized and chaotic mind to a mind that if happier, lighter, and feeling free.

Rehashing negative thoughts is only going to set you up for failure. It's important to start being mindful and recognize the kind of messages your brain is sending to itself. You might be taken aback to realize just how harmful a lot of the messages you send yourself are. Negativity is like a disease. Once it gets a hold of you, it will do its best to keep hanging around, refusing to let go. These thoughts are going to steadily ruin your success a little bit at a time if you don't do something to stop it. Thought replacement is the only effective technique needed to squash that inner critic inside you. The mind is a very powerful thing, and we can easily become a prisoner of our thoughts without even realizing that it is happening until it is too late. But that means that our minds are just as capable, just as strong enough to turn things around if we wanted it to. It's important to start acknowledging what you say to yourself. You're doing it all the time anyway, except we're not mindful of these thoughts. *Listen* to the way you talk to yourself. Once you begin noticing the messages you send, it's time to replace the less than desirable ones.

Every negative thought that is created in your mind can be transformed into something positive and constructive ones. To break the negativity loop, here's what you need to do:

- **Identify Them** - Pinpoint exactly what your unhelpful thoughts and separate them from the negative ones. Yes, there is a difference between the two. Not all negative thoughts are necessarily bad. An example of a negative thought is, "I'm stressed and frustrated, but I know it will get easier," while an unhelp thought would be, "I hate my current job and I never want to go back to that office again!". The unhelpful thoughts are the ones you want to focus on getting rid of.

- **Push Back Against Them** - Once you've identified what your unhelpful thoughts are, it's time to work on challenging them. Facts are going to be your greatest defense in this step. If they're not valid and based on facts, push back against these thoughts by focusing on the information that you know. Always go back to the facts that you know and cross-reference that with your thoughts. Ask yourself, *"Am I basing this on fact? Or speculation?"*. Replace these unhelpful thoughts with concrete facts to support your argument and make it believable. The facts never lie and focusing on this is one way of reigning in your thoughts to keep them from spiraling out of control.

- **Be Mindful of Them** - Watch the ongoing monologue that runs through your mind. Self-awareness about the nature of your self-talk is where you start making the necessary changes needed to change the way you think. When we're not mindful of the changes in our thoughts, the negativity makes us feel worse, and it becomes even more difficult to focus. By being mindful of the thoughts that creep into your head, you're instantly more attuned to what those thoughts are and how they make you feel. It if is bad for you or going to affect your confidence levels, you need to remove these thoughts from your life. For good.

- **Trade Them** - It can be hard to remain positive all the time, especially when you've experienced a setback or things are not going according to plan. However, try to trade your negative thoughts in for positive ones whenever you can. For example, instead of seeing setbacks as the end of the road, acknowledge that they can sometimes be opportunities in disguise. Instead of seeing failure as an indication that you're not good enough, see failure as a teacher you learn from. It all depends on how you look at it. Train your mind to look at this from a positive point of view. See the bright side and the good of every situation, and you will find that often things may not be as bleak as it initially seems.

Don't Be Afraid to Talk About It

As social creatures by nature, one of the unspoken things we yearn for is a deep connection to others. But in order to develop that deep connection, we must be able to openly share ourselves with others. We need to build enough trust to let others in, or we will always feel alone. Yet a lot of people hold back out of fear. They fear rejection, or they worry about how the other person might respond. They're afraid of being hurt and maybe they've had their heart broken in the past and they're scared to open up again.

As adults, the way we learn to perceive, handle and regulate emotions and feelings starts going downhill. Instead of learning how to deal with emotions in a healthy way, talk about our feelings, and express ourselves openly without fear of rejection, what we're being told instead is *suppress them* or. Phrases like *"You'll be fine, don't think about it," "get over it," "put on a brave face," "don't show emotion you'll be perceived as weak," "you're making too big a deal out of this,"* are all too common and they lead to one outcome: *The inability to properly manage your emotions let alone master them, which then leads to difficulty talking about it.* We've become so conditioned to think showing emotion a sign of weakness. People are uncomfortable talking about feelings and they're even uncomfortable *listening to someone else* talk about their feelings.

Everything you've learned in this book so far is meant to help you rewire your brain and change it, so you start living a happier, better, and more meaningful life the way you deserve. So, what can you do to learn to talk about your feelings more? Use the following guideline and take it one step at a time:

- **Unlock That Bottle** - Don't keep your emotions bottled up inside. Learn to be okay with expressing yourself and letting it all out. Your emotions are not your enemy, so start embracing them instead of resisting them. Don't forget that the brain has a limited storage space capacity. All those thoughts need to go somewhere, or they're going to get bigger and bigger, making it feel like your head is about to explode at the next trigger. Even if those emotions are uncomfortable or something you would prefer not to deal with, do it anyway because it is still a part of who you are.

- **Do What the Motivational Speakers Do -** At every opportunity, preach positivity. Imagine you're like a motivational speaker, and it's now your mission to spread positivity at every chance you get. Especially when you're interacting with someone who needs it and who may be struggling to overcome negativity too. You may not be a motivational speaker in a professional capacity, but that doesn't mean you can't take a leaf out of their book and preach and teach too. If your mind is capable of complaining and being negative without even thinking about it, you can certainly change your brain and your thoughts, so it goes in the opposite direction too.

- **Tell Them What You Want Them to Do -** Sometimes, all you need is someone to listen to you talk about your feelings or what's on your mind. without any judgment, criticism, or opinion. You just want them *to listen,* and that's okay. Let them know what you need from them right up front so they're on the same page.

Tell them *exactly* how you would like them to respond by saying this: *"I want to share something with you, I hope that's okay, but I just want you to listen because I'm not ready to solve this problem yet. I need to get it off my chest but that's all I feel ready for right now"*. Tell them right from the beginning and you'll find that your loved ones will be more than happy to meet your request. It takes away some of the fear of talking about it once you see that people are more than happy to meet you where you need them to. All you have to do sometimes is ask.

Conclusion

Thank you for making it through to the end of *Change Your Brain*, let's hope it was informative and able to provide you with all of the tools you need to achieve your goals whatever they may be.

Changing your brain for a better life, no doubt takes a lot of work. Even harder to break out of these unhelpful thought patterns and bad habits when you're dealing with anxiety too. But you've already made great progress by learning how the brain works and why we're wired to do or think in a certain way. Understanding is the first step toward overcoming any obstacle, including trying to change years of bad habits that have done nothing so far but keep you from achieving your goals.

Now that you're equipped with the tools you need to make the transformation, it's important that you start slow. Trying to do too much too soon is how a lot of people crash and burn. You need to start small, and this can't be emphasized enough. Yes, it seems like slow progress in the beginning, but that's okay. *Slow and steady wins the race.* It's about keeping your eye on the big picture and being patient with yourself along the way.

Any change that is worth it is going to require that you work for it.

The brain you have is *not the brain you're meant to have* for the rest of your life. The human brain is an incredibly powerful organ. With consistent practice, it can change. You know what you need to do. The rest, as they say, as up to you.

Finally, if you found this book useful in any way, a review on Amazon is always appreciated!

CPSIA information can be obtained
at www.ICGtesting.com
Printed in the USA
LVHW030349301120
673004LV00032B/497